Pink Harvest

FIRST SERIES: CREATIVE NONFICTION

PINK HARVEST

< Tales of Happenstance >

TONI MIROSEVICH

MID-LIST PRESS
Minneapolis

Mid-List Press publishes books of high literary merit and fresh artistic vision by new and
emerging writers and by writers ignored, marginalized, or excluded from publication by
commercial and mainstream publishers. Mid-List seeks to increase access to publication for
new writers, to nurture the growth of emerging writers, and to increase the diversity of books,
authors, and readers. Mid-List is a tax-exempt, 501(c)(3), not-for-profit literary organization.

Library of Congress Cataloging-in-Publication Data

Mirosevich, Toni.

  Pink harvest : tales of happenstance / Toni Mirosevich.

    p. cm. -- (First series--creative nonfiction)

  ISBN 978-0-922811-75-5 (pbk. : alk. paper)

  I. Title.

PS3563.I716Z46 2007

813'.54—dc22

                          2007034991

Printed in the United States of America

First printing: November 2007

Cover design: Philip Krayna

Cover photo: Seattle Post-Intelligencer Collection, Museum of History and Industry, Seattle, Washington

Text design: Lane Stiles

Grateful acknowledgment is made to the publications in which the following pieces, sometimes in
different form, previously appeared: *Bellevue Literary Review:* "The Raft"; *Best American Travel Writing—
2002* (Houghton Mifflin): "Lambs of God and the New Math"; *Five Fingers Review:* "The View";
Gastronomica: "The Prize Inside"; *Harrington Lesbian Fiction Quarterly:* "Letter from Croatia:
Bog i Hrvati," "At the Desk Where I Didn't Write, In the Room Where I Didn't Paint"; *modern words:*
"Pinball"; *My Oblique Strategies* (Thorngate Road, 2005): "Sx, Pl and the Gd Lf"; *Puerto Del Sol:*
"Near Vermeer"; *Queer Street* (Custom Words, 2005): "Pinball," "Near Vermeer," "The Windy City,"
"The Raft"; *San Francisco Chronicle Magazine:* "Lambs of God and the New Math," "The Windy City,"
"Kith and Kin," "The Bullet," "The Hot Spot"; *Santa Clara Review:* "Truant"; *Santa Monica Review:*
"The Nutria," "The Road to Shalimar"; *The Rooms We Make Our Own* (Firebrand Books, 1996):
"Pink Harvest"; *Transfer:* "Tilting"; *Western Humanities Review:* "The Whole Story"; *Zyzzyva:*
"Digging," "Long Live Our Side."

In memory of my father, Tony Mirosevich,
and for my mother, Pearl Skifich Mirosevich

Contents

Acknowledgments

To the following people who helped bring in the *Pink Harvest*, my gratitude and love: Carol Brewer and Linda Trunzo, Susan Mirosevich Bahl, Marny Hall, Frances Mayes, Nona Caspers, Glenda Grider, David Mallory of Morningstar Fisheries (Princeton, California), the Faheys, Carolyn Chute, and Valerie Trueblood. For their generosity and guidance, I also wish to thank Marianne Nora and Lane Stiles, Mary Logue, Alison Biggar, Carolyn J. Marr at the Museum of History and Industry (Seattle, Washington), and Philip Krayna for his skill in bringing the original 1958 black-and-white cover photo to life. Fellowships with the MacDowell Colony, the Willard R. Espy Literary Foundation, and the Djerassi Resident Artists Program supported the writing of this book.

And to Shotsy Faust, with abiding love.

< *ix* >

The View

SPILLOVER. THAT'S WHAT OCCURRED WHEN THE EMERGENCY room could take no more, when those yet to be seen would remain unseen. The pain in the chest. The cough that persisted. The *Say, Nurse, I got this hurt in my side,* and no doctor available to lift the flannel shirt and attend to the knife wound, fresh and ragged.

When the emergency room was packed, the gurneys racing by like go-carts or city buses filled to the max, and though you've waited and waited for hours for a bus to stop, the bus roars by, then it was off to Urgent Care, a clinic at the other end of the hospital, to deal with the spillover, where a doctor, a nurse practitioner, a nurse, a medical assistant, and a security guard—the bouncer at the bar—saw whomever dropped in for whatever ailment.

The beginning of the month was always slow. After the first, when the checks came in, the junkies were too busy scoring, the transactions fast and furious on the street, and for the others, who knows. Maybe everything appears more hopeful at the start of a month and anything that is acute seems less acute, and all a person needs is occasional care or lackadaisical care or less than urgent, Urgent Care. But by the end of the month, when the money runs out, when there is no food, no drugs, and there is nothing to numb you from your life, your life spills over, and for an instant you begin to see what brought you here, to this set of circumstances, this bottom rung. That's when everyone came streaming in, wanting this, seeking that, and the team dispensed and bandaged and listened and kicked out and saw as many as they could from when they opened at noon until they closed at eight. The day went quickly, but still, the day was long.

⚓   ⚓   ⚓

It was a typical day at Urgent Care, near the end of the month of December, typical except for the fact that it was December 23rd, two days before Christmas. Everyone who came in was at wit's end because, in truth, there is little wit left when there are no presents under the tree, there is no tree, and yes, while there is a free meal down at the mission, there is always that, still there's a need for something else to buffer, to ease the blow of Christmas coming round the bend, coming too quickly and no place to go.

That day all the people who came to clinic had a story, some well developed, some sketched out, some with quite a few key details missing. There was a woman who wanted the morning-after pill. The night before, at the bar, she decided, what the hell, it was close to the holidays, and went home with the guy buying drinks, but the next morning, when she woke up with this new Santa, she decided no, she wasn't ready to bring another elf into the world. There was a French tourist who lost his luggage, and tucked inside his suitcase was his shaving kit, and inside the kit his diabetes meds, and they were able to give him a new script and prevent diabetic shock. There was a housepainter who came in already lit, who wanted painkillers, for see, he had fallen off this scaffolding and hurt his back, but to tell the truth, he'd been hurting ever since his wife died two years ago, unexpectedly, out of the blue, and since then he'd been in a lot of pain, and couldn't they give him something, something to help him through the holidays, something to help him get over the hump?

They saw forty patients that day, a normal load given the quick do-si-do of managed care. The nurse—who was feeling festive—brought in a boom box and some Christmas tunes, Elvis's "Blue Christmas," and "Jingle Bell Rock," and she threw in Coltrane's "A Love Supreme," perhaps the best Christmas song of all time. Near the end of the shift, around dinnertime, someone ordered out for pizza and all in all it wasn't a bad day but by eight o'clock they were tired and ready to go home to their families and maybe start Christmas early, have a little nog, and that's when the nurse practitioner noticed one more chart on the door, and when she looked in the waiting room saw one more man.

He was homeless. There were all the external signs, the visual clues that go with that word, that accumulate around that word like dust accumulates around an unused thing, a houseplant or knickknack, something that stays in one place and does not move. He had a navy knit cap pulled down low on his forehead that kept his head warm and controlled his dreads. He was wearing a khaki army coat with rips down the front and sleeves and baggy jeans and he reeked of urine and other smells, smoke and mold and a must that smells like the corner of a closet where no fresh air has gotten in. He sat there in a plastic orange chair, in the fluorescent light of the waiting room, holding one hand up, bent in on his chest, like a dog holds up a hurt paw. When she went to him (yes, she would take him, even though it was the end of the shift), his first words were, "I'm terribly sorry, ma'am. I know it's late and this is an awful inconvenience for you but I was wondering if you would be so kind as to take a look at my hand."

She was surprised by his diction, how articulate, how gracious, for even after twenty years of this kind of work she still had assumptions about people. She assumed that his speech would be slurred or that the con would be on or he would be full of invective, angry at the world and at her, the latest messenger from that world. But the man spoke softly and each word was well placed and he went on to tell her that the same thing, the thing with the hand, had happened a few months ago and a doctor at a free clinic said he might have some form of palsy. She had seen this presentation before, the hand curled in like a baby, the telltale sign of drunks who fall asleep on the street, on the pavement, in that position, and she knew that sometimes the hand straightens out and sometimes not.

"You've been sleeping on the street?" she asked, though she already knew the answer, and he answered well yes, recently he'd been down on his luck, but this was a temporary condition. She said, "I can get you some clothes and a place in a shelter for the night," she could pull some strings, and he said, "Well, no, thank you," for he thought he'd be staying in the neighborhood for a while around till, well, maybe February, and that he'd be fine.

As there was nothing she could do for his hand she asked, "When did you last have something to eat?" and he said, "Well, I had a little something, yesterday, I think," and she asked, "Would you like some pizza?" and he said, "Well, thank you, yes, I could do with a slice." So she went out of the room and brought him back a piece. She turned her back while he ate for it's impolite to stare and suddenly she was on her best behavior, remembering etiquette her mother taught her many years ago.

The room was quiet, so quiet she heard the wall clock tick. She looked up and saw that it was eight-thirty, a half-hour past closing, and knew that outside in the hall the security guard was fidgeting, the medical assistant cursing under his breath, *Come on, come on, let's go.* But she would not rush the man. When he finished eating he rose from his chair and as he was turning to go he hesitated and then he said, "I hate to bother you any further but might it be possible to get a little Bacitracin? I have a little infection, a little hole in my side, and that seems to help."

And she thought, *Oh, no, I need to look at this,* and asked him if she could.

He got back up on the exam table and removed his ripped jacket, then the black sweater under it, and then the torn brown work shirt under that. When he got down to his T-shirt, the last layer, he lifted it up and there, on the left side of his chest, where the skin should cover, there was a hole, a large round hole in the side of his chest.

She knelt down to look. The hole went in for about two inches and created a framed scene like a shadow box. She peered inside. Where there once were ribs there were no ribs. Nothing to block the view, nothing like the tall overgrown pine tree in her neighbor's yard that obscured her peek of the ocean. It was as if the timbers of the body had been cut away. Farther inside the hole, she saw what looked like a membrane, pink, almost opaque, like a thin clear sheet, which contrasted with his dark brown skin. A thin, thin pink sheet through which she could see the outline of what lay beyond the sheet. First she saw his lungs breathing. Then she could see straight inside to the man's heart.

For as long as she remembered she'd always wanted to see what was inside of a person. She imagined herself a different type of explorer, different from Admiral Byrd or Lewis and Clark. She wanted to find an inside passage, cut a slim opening around the heart, a little porthole to see inside, to see what lived there: rancor or love, to see whether the person was big-hearted or small, had a heart the size of a melon or a pea. What if you could see what had wrapped around the heart, love's strings or cancer or anything we can't name? What if you could look inside to see whether your loved one's heart was true blue, its color soft and glacial? She pictured a viewfinder, a roll of dimes, a crowd of people waiting to see.

When she found her voice again she said, "Listen, I've never seen anything like this. Do you mind if I show my colleagues?" for this was a teaching hospital, and he waved his hand and said, "Oh no, that's fine, I know this is important to you people, you people always want to see the view," and then he went on to explain what had happened. He had been diagnosed with a rare infection in his lungs and a year ago a doctor had performed a one-of-a-kind operation to remove the infection. He had to take out a section of ribs to do it. That seemed to work out fine except that sometimes the rim around the hole got a little infected, and now she noticed the red inflamed area around the opening, the irritated sash of the window.

She asked him to wait and had the doctor and the nurse and the med assistant and a resident from another clinic come in. They looked in at his heart and he was gracious and said, "I know, I know, this is how you learn," but all the while they were looking in she wondered how he knew this is what they needed to learn.

Maybe each person saw something different, depending on what his or her own heart held. If your heart was full of joy you saw reflected delight. If your heart was full of bitterness, reflected enmity. Maybe the doctor saw a heart wrapped in thorns and maybe the med tech a heart tied with a lavender ribbon. Maybe some looked in as you might look in the window of an Easter egg and saw a little scene—a house by a lake, and swans or lily pads—and maybe others saw nothing, nothing at all.

Or a bridal veil or a vale of tears. A handshake. A ship's bell. A love note. A target. A red zone.

After the others left, she took down the antiseptic ointment from the shelf and applied some of the unguent to his skin around the opening, then asked him to dress and went out to write up his chart. It took her a few minutes to write the history, for she kept getting off track and writing down what wasn't essential, imagining what brought him here, on this night, at this particular intersection of time and place, giving meaning to his visit, then erasing meaning, and then imagining where he would go, the hospital grounds or the freeway ramps nearby. What would become of him, what would he eat the next day and the next? Would the view inside change with time? Would the hole ever close?

She put the last note in the file and went back to the exam room. He was already gone. She'd wanted to say something more, to give him something, something to place over the hole to protect what was inside. She locked the door to the room and walked out to the waiting room.

The lights were still on. There, sitting off to one corner, were the nurse and the man. Their backs were to her and their heads were bent down as if they were praying. But as she walked towards them she could see their hands were moving. They seemed to be involved in some project. They did not notice her.

She saw the man hold the roll of tape while the nurse pulled a length off. The nurse cut a long length from the roll and applied the strip to one of the tears in his coat. She sat down beside them and help applied the rest. For if they couldn't fix the hole in his side, they fixed what they could, the holes in his jacket where the wind blew through, for he had fewer layers than most and like all of us, he needed some extra cover.

The Whole Story

There must be some reason why we look
where we look when we look.

—*Last Orders*, Graham Swift

IT WAS A RECONCILIATION DINNER OF SORTS.

To tell the whole story of how two couples fell away from each other, how the cold war started, would be to recount all the little things that build over time, small affronts, insensitivities, to recall that the first slight was easily forgiven; you simply thought that the other couple didn't realize that bringing a lone pineapple to your birthday party, grabbed off the kitchen shelf at the last minute, would upset you. At the time you rationalized, "Birthdays are less important to them than to me," and when you received the gift said, "Oh, I adore pineapple," yet to tell the whole story would be to remember that a month later you didn't attend one of the pair's birthday party, made up an excuse, and then, a month after that, there was their last-minute cancellation of dinner plans after you had slaved all day over a chocolate gateau. By that time none of it was a surprise, for each of us had started keeping a tally, keeping score, for a tally begs a listing, a tally always grows, soon you were on the lookout for something, anything that could be misconstrued and added to the list.

When a tally is long, detailed, cross-indexed, there must be a final straw, in this case the evening they dropped by unexpectedly. Your dogs started barking, you yelled at them to stop, and out of nowhere one of the couple said, "My God, you are being so abusive to your animals." And that was it. You never called again.

So to tell how it came to be that two couples who once went away on weekends together, who once shared a river cabin where, in the middle of one night, a bat flew in through an attic window and all the women jumped out of bed, grabbed whatever they could find—brooms, umbrellas, spatulas—and ran around the small cabin in their underwear, implements aloft, yelling *Shoo, bat, shoo* to the tune of "Skip to My Lou," how these couples who had shared times like that had now not broken bread together for over five years, a long loop of time: it would take years to explain, so why not simply say they were on the outs, deeply estranged, and leave it at that?

Because to leave it at that would be to leave out what happened during the estrangement. During the years of not seeing them you began saying the Lord's Prayer again, for no initial reason whatsoever, just a feeling that took hold. You began saying it when you went to sleep at night, to help you to sleep at night, not because once, on a country back road, you saw a sign on a church billboard that read: GOD RESPONDS TO KNEE MAIL. The prayer was easy to remember; you said it silently so as not to wake your girlfriend and have to explain, and soon you found yourself giving special emphasis to one line in particular, as if yellow-highlighting one passage in the night: *and forgive us our trespasses as we forgive those who trespass against us.* What now made you pay attention to the first part of that line, the self-admission snuck in there, the realization that, lo and behold, you trespassed also, daily, consciously and unconsciously, that you had been an insensitive soul more times than you could count? Yesterday there was the person you cut off in traffic. You quickly mimed *I'm sorry* in the rearview mirror and thought that would do. You didn't call back the coworker whose husband was having the affair, for there was nothing new you could offer to ease her tale of woe and she'd survive. A tally, now with a different name at the top of the page, began to grow and you thought to yourself, wasn't it the poet Wallace Stevens who wrote *The house was quiet and the list was long*? You look it up in his *Collected Works* and see it's really "The world was quiet and the house was calm," but you prefer your version.

All of this—the tallying, the breakup, the estrangement, the Lord's Prayer said with special emphasis—would have continued for years without end, except that:

> One day, in late summer, one of the pair, an artist, sends a postcard announcing an opening for her new show. You go to the show, a show of faith, and once there you stand around, awkwardly, self-consciously, looking at the art pieces yet not really paying attention to the details, the color, the shapes and forms, conscious only of these friends, these human forms standing next to you whom you had once known and loved and shared so many things with, not the least of which was the bat weekend. While you are standing there you look for physical changes during those five years of absence—A little more graying at the temples? A shift in weight?—but notice instead

the way the body, whether with weight gain or loss, with age or infirmity, stands the same. There's the same posture, the same stance, as identifiable as the smallpox vaccine all of us of a certain age carry on the upper arm, that cluster of points that never alters and won't go away.

Afterwards, who could predict that the one who isn't an artist would apologize in the parking lot for whatever had occurred so long ago by saying, "I'm sure it was all my fault," and that you, who so wanted to hear those words, would say, sheepishly, "Let's have dinner soon." Isn't that what we all want to hear when others have hurt us inadvertently, unintentionally, have been as clueless as custard? Don't we wish to hear someone say, "I'm sure it was all my fault?" There are redemptive literary models, which offer reconciliation, like Dickens's example of forgiveness, that mess of neuroses, Little Dorrit, who said, "It's nobody's fault." Yet, my guess is that if Little Dorrit had an option, if she'd gone to therapy after debtor's prison, she might have sung a different tune. Something like, "Blameless? Few people are."

"Let's have dinner soon" is what you say, and here it is, the night of the dinner.

⚓ ⚓ ⚓

Over dinner and a few glasses of wine, I ask the artist what she is up to now. Based on what I saw at the art show she has shifted from working with clay—black Nelson-like structures, coal-black platforms and towers, stacks and columns—to portraiture. They are semi-abstract portraits, of her girlfriend, of coworkers, a couple of self-portraits, all done in dark, thick colors. She's returned to the human figure. Portraiture may signal a switch back to basics, that need artists sometimes feel to return to their beginnings, the early attempts to render the muscles, the sinews, the torso, the hands; all that comprises the glorious human form.

And here they are, before us, raising their glasses in the golden light of the table lamp, alive in their glorious human forms, and I am suddenly overcome and have to make an excuse to leave the table and busy myself at the kitchen sink.

Fuck the pineapple. I have missed them. Deeply.

As I refill her wineglass the artist says that since the show she's enrolled in a new painting class, then adds that she's acquired a new device to help her paint.

New brushes, perhaps? After working with clay so many years, maybe a wristbrace?

She reaches into her sweater pocket and takes out a small rectangular plastic box with a tiny screen. A new, top-of-the-line Palm Pilot.

"Every morning," she says, "I get up and turn on the computer at home and download all kinds of stuff onto the Palm: headlines from the *New York Times* and newspapers from around the world, recipes, the Dow. I can access all of it, anywhere, on the bus, at the grocery, at the Laundromat."

She doesn't play the market. She doesn't cook. She rarely discusses world affairs. I picture her in all the places she's named, peering down at the small screen, accessing away.

I still don't quite get the draw until she reveals that the Palm has a special feature, a small camera inside with an itsy photo lens that looks like a tiny suction cup. At any moment of the day or night she can click and shoot what catches her eye.

She gives us a demonstration. As I lift the heel of the baguette to my mouth, she clicks. When my girlfriend takes a sip of wine, she clicks. When her girlfriend piles risotto high on her fork and performs a high-wire act from fork to mouth, she clicks. She swivels around in her chair and takes pictures of our new puppy and our old dog, the dog that wasn't old the last time they came to dinner. The old dog recognized them when they came in, remembered their smell, then looked at us as if to say, *For Christ's sake, we can't wait for protracted reconciliation! Time goes by more quickly for us! Thank Lassie, someone apologized!*

She tells us she uses the handheld to shoot a photo gallery of random people who cross her path during the day. In the evening she hooks the Palm up to the computer, downloads the day's contents, then decides which to keep and which to turf, which portrait she will transfer from the interior to the exterior, from screen to canvas.

I wonder how this adds to or alters the final work, this extra set of steps and stages, the transfer of living image to technological image to canvas, a non-technological medium. Replication after replication. Once I knew a writer who first wrote his stories in longhand, then typed them on an old Royal, then input them on the computer, and finally printed them out and revised with red pen. He said that each step added something to the final story as each medium was different. I thought it sounded interesting so I gave it a shot. It took me six months to write a paragraph so I abandoned the process.

As I watch her scan the room I have to admit, it's a good project given her innate talent for capturing the ephemeral, the dynamic moment. Her keen eye was the first to see the bat. Still, I wonder what happens in the instant, what flash of intuition causes her to point the camera, to click and shoot. So much is contained in the moment, so much goes into it, a combination of the light, what finds its way into the lens, how hungry you are, the decision to stay a moment longer on the square or go get a slice of pizza, how happy you are, how melancholy and unable to take any more in, no matter how beautiful the light on the square or the pizza, how itchy the trigger finger, whether you are still thinking about the slight five years ago. *You* thought the pineapple was a fine gift. All of this factors in, doesn't it? And what did she do before this new innovation—where and how were the images retained? If the Palm effectively records what was present and is now past, if it takes the place of memory, what is lost? When you see sunlight on a palm tree, the combination of feelings and thoughts at that moment in time makes you see the palm as big as a barn or as small as a postage stamp. Then you only have the photo lens of your mind's eye to record the image and carry it with you. Memory, with the aid of the imagination, works then as a valise, a carryall, an overnight suitcase of images we carry along on our daily travels. A bag of needments. Those images are as necessary as the spare underwear, pajamas, the socks and toiletries. Now, so much of that is contained in a small plastic rectangle.

The implications are frightening. Will the imagination and memory atrophy from lack of use, as the muscles atrophy from the sedentary life?

⚓   ⚓   ⚓

She begins to tell us a story. The other night, in her painting class, the teacher started talking about Francis Bacon and the series he painted entitled *After Van Gogh.* In the series, van Gogh is walking into the fields, on his way to view and paint the countryside. The paintings are modeled after a series of self-portraits van Gogh did of this very walk, which were destroyed. How, we can only guess, for when I inquire I find she has forgotten the whole story. She does know that Bacon decided to replicate the originals, the paintings that were destroyed, in his own idiosyncratic style. Somewhere I have seen these paintings but I can't quite recall where or when. Maybe, years ago, I looked up Bacon on her recommendation.

"As the teacher was talking I remembered one painting in particular from the series. It was my favorite, *is* my favorite, maybe of all time. When I was twenty I traveled to New York and saw it at MOMA. I remember every detail. In the painting van Gogh is walking down a yellow path, through dark orange and red fields. All the colors are deep, oversaturated. The sky is a blue I've rarely seen captured, a blue you could fall through into something else. A sky like a false ceiling."

That was thirty years ago. I try to imagine her at twenty, youthful, impressionable. What preceded that moment of intense viewing? What, in her life, led up to that desire to truly see for the first time? She grew up in Pittsburgh, across from the steel mills. The spectacle she witnessed daily from her bedroom window was a line of dark gray smokestacks, a black-soot sky. The city's limited color palette. To see Bacon's paintings, to have color wash over her visual field must have been life-altering, must have felt like a celebration, a holiday, like the lighted cellophane wheel that spins and washes color over an aluminum Christmas tree, turning it from silver to red to yellow to blue.

"It was that very painting, that introduction to the fields, to color, that made me decide I wanted to become an artist. That was the moment. I stood in front of that painting and wept. I didn't know why. I stood there until the place closed down and the docents escorted me out the door."

So there it was, the turning point. She stood in front of a painting and for the first time in her life looked deeply, intently, and was transformed by a portrait of a painter walking out into the fields. Wasn't this also van Gogh's intention, to observe, to look deeply, to fall into the deep meditation that is looking, so necessary for the creation of art? I can see the image of him, walking stick in one hand, easel in another, straw hat, red beard, walking out into a field of red and orange. I picture the painting as if I saw it yesterday.

I pour some more wine. I can tell there is more to the story. She has only given us the sketch, the pencil drawing, the outline.

"So I go home that night from painting class and it's late, but I decide to look at the photos from the day." She picks up the Palm from the table and holds it preciously, like a Fabergé egg. "I still have that series of pictures on here."

The four of us gather around the tiny black-and-white screen. She boots up and the photos begin to appear, grainy, but visible.

There is a picture of her girlfriend, in bed, propped up against the pillow, not fully awake and looking slightly miffed. Then some people she met during that day, a guy arranging a display of mangoes at the Farmer's Market, a young woman in a plaid car coat boarding a bus. A businessman walking down Market Street.

"Look at that one," she says, pointing to the man, not clicking to the next frame.

There is nothing extraordinary about the picture. A nondescript businessman, most likely on his lunch hour, walking toward something, a meeting, a lunch date, a croissant sandwich. Maybe this is a game we'll play, trying to guess where he is going. Of all the people she could have chosen to capture, why stop at this man, unknown to her, unconnected, "a suit," the title she gave all businessmen, not even someone she could relate to?

"Look again."

He is walking head down. He is wearing a fedora, the current fashion statement of men in downtown San Francisco. In his left hand he carries a briefcase, in his right a cell phone. He is walking somewhere.

I know I am missing something. She observes me while I observe the screen. This is a test of some sort, a test of whether we can be friends again. I look at the sidewalk, at the newspaper blowing into a ditch, at the buildings in the background. At the woman stepping off the curb behind the man. At the man once again. On his way to somewhere. In his left hand a briefcase, in his right hand a cell phone.

In his left hand an easel, in his right hand a walking stick.

It is the exact same pose, position, silhouette, the very same stance as van Gogh walking into the French countryside. What she has captured is the modern-day equivalent of the painter walking into the field, painted by van Gogh, then by Francis Bacon, another painter with an easel in hand. Now, in present day, our friend is about to do the same, to paint this image, an image she saw thirty years ago in a museum.

If you were to film the sequence, over time, if would look like an Escher painting, a hand painting a hand painting a hand.

She stops, the length of a shutter click. "I took this shot that morning, before the class met. Before the teacher ever mentioned van Gogh."

This random shot was taken before the lecture, before the evening when the teacher would make her recall the painting, before the memory was triggered. The image was living in her; she had been carrying it with her all these years, as we carry with us that which we love and cannot part with, as we had been carrying pictures of these friends. The pineapple birthday. The time of the bats. The time we went out to eat at North Beach and parked on a hill and my girlfriend slipped and her entire body slid under the car. She was there and then she wasn't. The time we all were broke and decorated a Christmas tree with white plastic forks and knives and pasted a picture of the baby Jesus on a paper plate for the star. The time we stood together looking at something—at films, at the dogs, at each other. All of these images held in the body, in the memory, over time.

How did it occur? Why this look and not that? This moment and not that? Why did she focus on the man with the hat instead of the woman stepping off the curb behind him? Why the return to portraiture and the choice to pick that painting class and the decision by the teacher to bring up Bacon on that evening and the idea thirty years ago to travel to New York to see an art exhibit at MOMA and expand one's worldview from black-and-white to color? Why the idea to purchase a Palm Pilot, which allowed her to carry images with her like a valise or a briefcase or a paint-box that contains all the colors you need to transform the world, a paint-box like Vincent also carried with him that day to replicate the images of the fields?

The story could stop there, but it wouldn't be the whole story.

There is something else I can't get at. Why does the man in the photo look weirdly familiar? I have seen this all before, the painting as she was describing it, the colors, the fields, retained as if it were I, not she, who was at MOMA, as if I were overcome, as if I were taking the painting class, and had snapped the picture of the man on the street, that it had all reverberated inside of me.

I have a sense of vertigo—from the wine? the image?—and the room spins. I look past the table to the bookshelves that line the living room, where all the other images are kept, all the written, photographic, artistic images in these books, shelves and shelves of rectangles. This is where all the information resided before computers, Palm Pilots, and the like. My eyes fall on a brown oversized book with gold-embossed letters. I can't quite read the title from where I am sitting so I excuse myself and say I want to open the living-room window for some air. As I pass by the book I lean in and read the gold script on the spine: FRANCIS BACON.

It's a battered book on Francis Bacon. The old dog, when he was puppy, chewed the spine off at one end.

Here it is, what we have kept and not returned. What we have kept and couldn't give back, as we hold on to memories, unwilling or unable to release them, for to lose them would be to add to the tally of all that's been lost and estrangement is a long channel of choppy water which no boat can cross, nothing can be sent and nothing can be returned.

I know what the book holds. At this very moment, the very same painting that moved her so long ago, the one that we have seen tonight in our imaginations, is resting but ten feet from the table where we sit.

I consider my options. I could lift the book off the shelf. I could say, *Oh my God, what a coincidence, here's a book I'd forgotten we had on Bacon,* and, an appropriate second or two later, *Look, it has your name on the inside cover, it must be your book, isn't that strange?* And then, after nonchalantly leafing through, *Oh, look, isn't this the very painting we've been talking about?* But I don't. For to do that would be to acknowledge this trespass, this sin, to acknowledge that everywhere you look is a reminder of the past that returns whether you want it to or not, it is the same form, the same shape, here is van Gogh, over and over again, here on the street, in the painting class, and here, too, in this very room.

This trespass. This sin.

But the house is quiet and the list is long. How can we trust that the reconciliation will stick, that we will ever get to share these stories again? What if holding on to the book all these years is enough to sever the tenuous bond, so fragile, so just forming, the dog-chewed spine seen as an example of how we were cavalier about what was important to them, and didn't care. Like a pineapple. Like a chocolate gateau.

We will never know the whole story. Of why one person apologized. Of why another kept a book. Of why van Gogh chose that spectacle over another or why Bacon seemed driven to replicate what was once destroyed. The only thing we can hope for is to know the partial story, and then be left to wonder at the need for estrangement, at the long loop of time, at the chance of reconciliation that presents itself, not so often, not often enough in the short life of dogs. We may also never know all the layers on which reconciliation occurs, the layers like thick layers of paint, for there is not only the physical reconciliation of long-parted friends, all of us once again together in a room, but the reconciliation that happens, unplanned, unscripted, with memory, held in the imagination as an image is held in a Palm. A memory of a younger body, a more youthful time, a reconciliation between who we were then and who we are now.

If a prayer is remembered because it was repeated over and over again when we were young and once gave solace, and years later is replicated again—*Our Father, Our Father, Our Father*—like a familiar lyric returning, a familiar cadence, aren't we experiencing not only a reconciliation with the past but also a reconciliation with the idea of forgiveness that the prayer offers, a reconciliation with comfort, a reconciliation with the body that said the prayer, all of these happening simultaneously, all as familiar as the replication over and over again of an image of a man walking forward, toward something we cannot see?

I return to the table empty-handed. The artist asks, "Do you mind if I take a picture, of all of us here?"

In a week or so I'll give them back the book.

Return. The four of us around the table, like so many times before, as if this picture of us were caught in the Palm, carried there.

These are the shapes we long for—these familiar shapes. Here we are, in the same positions, gathered around the table; one holding a glass, one looking at the light, one reaching to pet a dog, one viewing the spectacle from a distance, on a small, tiny screen.

Near Vermeer

TO FRAME A PAINTING OR AN IMAGE—AS VERMEER MIGHT have done if given this scene, a crowded dining room of a local Chinese restaurant—first you must block out all the surrounding activity: the waiters, officious in their black vests and pants, bent ever so slightly at the waist, leaning toward the tables, pens poised to take orders, as if about to pen a letter; the women, designated handmaidens, weaving in and out of traffic, balancing serving trays to deliver shark fin soup or honey-baked sea bass or tender greens; one runs by with a tray full of small cups of rice, uniform mounds, a perfect mountain range of twelve rounded peaks.

If you are an artist (unlike my girlfriend, Shots, and I, two women out to a Chinese restaurant after a day of painting a room), you must block out the customers coming in—those waiting impatiently in the restaurant foyer, their physical relief as they shuck off their coats, block out the sound of chairs scraping back, the longed-for signal by the hostess, a wave of her hand: "Here, this table is yours."

Next, block out the man and woman at the table behind you, seated across from each other, owners or managers who do not serve, who count packets of greenbacks with their eyes trained on each other's hands. Each eyes the quick shuffle of green, to check, to assure there's no mischief. The scene has all the staged intensity of an old-fashioned bank heist: the bundles of twenties, the thick rubber bands, the count.

In a painting, the frame would block out all this activity, these distractions, much like Vermeer blocked out what was behind, below, above *The Girl Reading a Letter at an Open Window,* offering only her face, her upper torso, the sunlight pouring in. He chose to edit all that resides outside the frame, as if to say, this is what the world should look like. We, as viewers, cannot see beyond what we see, must imagine whether the girl has a crutch propped up against the table, or children, out of view, screaming for bowls of porridge, or a husband coming in the doorway demanding service. We can only see her face, her torso, the letter. What did he decide was unimportant? What lies in the corner that we're not supposed to see? What does the letter say?

Here you must make a conscious effort to exclude. An artist has not intervened. The eye must erase all that is extraneous in the visual field:

the banquet tables, each with a lazy Susan spinning in the center, the large bottles of Coke and 7-Up at the ready. The staged elements of this interior—the plastic bamboo trees, plastic tiles of a pitched roof, rice-paper screens—are placed to suggest that we are in a garden courtyard in China and not in a large stucco building off the main freeway to the airport next to a Blockbuster. You must erase the fake rockery, the fake koi pond, forget the pretense that it is fed by a natural spring, remove the very real fish, orange and speckled, moving sluggishly in the small cramped pool.

Once you address the details of the larger sphere, you can focus on a smaller circle, the table six feet away from yours, the five people seated there: two couples, middle aged, in their late thirties or early forties, and one boy. Remove the two men from view, the other woman. Everything must go except the boy and his mother. Given that, just the mention of a boy and his mother at a restaurant table, where would you place them? Seated next to each other? Would you imagine a young child pulling on his mother's sleeve, wanting more rice or attention or something else, something he needs that he cannot name?

Focus in, but try to be discreet. Of the Vermeer painting a critic wrote, "She is alone in an unguarded moment, unviolated by the intrusion of the viewer." Here too you don't wish to intrude and make them self-conscious.

How can she not be self-conscious?

She sits at the table wearing a gray fleece sweatshirt and jeans. She is talking to the other adults. Her boy could hardly be called a child. Already he has grown past the age we would designate as childhood by certain visual indicators: his length of limb, his unlaced tennis shoes—huge, teenage-sized—the loss of a child's facial features, that absence of calculation we see on, say, a five-year-old face, a lack of calculation we sometimes associate with those who are deemed slow—as if calculation were a measure of maturity.

He is twelve, or close to. He is sitting on her lap. He is cradled in his mother's arms, curled up, facing her, his head resting or lolling against her right shoulder, moving very slightly, up and down, as he breathes. She is holding him as if he were a suckling infant, as if he has yet to know the power of his limbs, is not strong enough or capable enough to trust in his limbs, like a child who has not yet learned to walk. He needs to be held, more than most infants, and he sleeps in her arms. She continues her conversation with the others as if there is nothing amiss, as if she is oblivious to all around her. Her visual field stops at table's edge, like the girl in the painting who sees only the letter, who remains oblivious to the children, the husband, the crutch.

Or maybe she is conscious of all around her and has chosen what to leave out; the quick brushstrokes, a flash of green at the manager's table, splash of orange in the pond, the hostess rushing by with a patron's coat, the waiter penning another order, or the strangers at the table next to hers, staring her way.

Is it only amiss to us, two women who have come out to treat ourselves to a celebratory dinner of snow crab, black bean oysters with pea shoots—we who did not expect the restaurant to be so full on a Tuesday night or to find, sitting next to us, a woman with her almost teenaged, and possibly retarded, son, carrying on as if it were normal to have a grown boy on her lap, at peace, gone to the world? Why should this seem amiss, this mother and child, and not the fake koi pond or the stack of money or the mountain range of rice?

If only we were looking downward, if our eyes were cast down upon our food, or staring straight ahead, oblivious to the fact that we are the only non-Asians in the restaurant, two women together, lovers, perhaps questionable in our affiliations. Quite possibly out of the restaurant's normal frame. If our eyes were on each other, on the pattern of paint splatter on our clothes, if we stopped at the border the table presents, our vision would be limited to that circumference, and not at what lies in the corner of the eye—their table next to us, six feet away, the woman, the boy soon to be a man, the rice bowls half full, the diffuse, nonspecific light. If I erased the sound the chairs make, the orders yelled out, all the conversations, the din, to listen to Shots's voice—lowered, hushed, so others will not hear—when she tells me that in many cultures there is shame in having a child who is born abnormal, as if it were the parent's failure, then I could hear her say that often parents choose to abandon these children or not have them at all. I could hear her say the world would be diminished without this boy's presence and others who make us expand our view beyond the frame.

"How can we know about frailty if the frail ones are left out?" she asks.

Earlier in the day, we painted the living room a golden yellow, a paint called "falling star," chosen for the warmth of the color, of the name, and chosen too so it would light the room on days when the outside world was dark and gray. We know that when we sit on the couch in this newly painted room the walls will cast a golden light on our faces, as if all the days outside are sunny, as if there is always light pouring in from an open window.

I turn to look at them again. There is no special light, no way her face or his is illuminated by the glow of the overhead fluorescents. No painter adds shadow or angle to give depth or dimension. There is no open window in this windowless room. The faces do not turn toward the late afternoon sun like four o'clocks or like morning glories turn toward a sunrise. Whatever light shines is interior, the mother's face turned inward toward her son, toward a vista without a mountain range, a smaller circumference. Everything else is removed: the pond, the rice, the tables, the waiters, us, all that is unnecessary.

Sx, Pl and the Gd Lf

SHE SHOWED ME HER TRANSCRIPT FROM HER COLLEGE DAYS, back in the sixties. I saw the "C" in Physics, the "A" in Art, the "B" in Humanities, then saw the "F"—the flunk, the fail—in Sx, Pl, and the Gd Lf.

What did the initials stand for? I asked. Six Philosophies and the Gold Leaf? Sauces, Pilafs, and the Garden Loaf? Sioux Politics and the Grand Left?

"Sex, Pleasure, and the Good Life," she muttered, and when I gave her a look she shot back, "I wasn't comin' to class. I was livin' it."

At the Desk Where I Didn't Write,
In the Room Where I Didn't Paint

SOMEHOW, IN THE COURSE OF THE EVENING, WE GET TO TALKING about junkies we have known. And old girlfriends. The two topics are not mutually exclusive.

My girlfriend, Shots, and I, a couple of long standing, are in the back seat of a car, being ferried to the movies by two good friends, also a couple of long standing. Earlier in the day, the four of us conferred on the phone and finally, by consensus, came up with a movie we could all tolerate, given our different sensibilities. We settled on *The Shipping News*, though I feared the movie version would flatten the original story. But it was that or a sci-fi thriller, a spy caper, or a film about corporate angst. A film about memory and loss in a cold, damp climate—so like the Northwest where three of us in the car are from—is the one we compromised on.

One of the couple in the front seat, Nina, is an old, old friend with whom my girlfriend and I have a history. We all three shared a semi-communal house in Seattle many years ago, a house where lovers switched back and forth and where we wrangled over collective decisions on what groceries to buy—tofu burgers or tofu hot dogs, wheat germ or wheat grass. We were all much younger and gayer then, more fit, more irresponsible. Now we are less fit, more settled. Every one of us has a regular job. Everyone in the car is sitting on a 401(k).

⚓   ⚓   ⚓

Nina and Joan arrived at our house thirty minutes late, and, in the rapid-fire delivery that often accompanies lateness, started explaining why. They had just come from spending a day purchasing paintbrushes for Joan, the one we never shared a house with. Joan is the identified creative one of the pair, an artist who doesn't drive. So all day Nina drove her from one art supply store to another, looking for just the right set of brushes for Joan's new project—a rogues' gallery of portraits, all of her friends from the neck up, sans torsos. Joan felt that the difference between using a cheap paintbrush and an excellent one was the difference between painting a one-dimensional mug and a face with the fine features and visual complexity of say, a Judi Dench, who was currently playing a lesbian, albeit a closeted lesbian in woolens, in *The Shipping News.*

After they'd searched and searched, Joan found brushes she really liked, with beautiful wooden handles and with bristles of some fine, indecipherable hair. She took the brushes up to the register and was shocked to find out they cost sixty dollars apiece. On impulse, she bought them. They are, at this very moment, lying in the trunk of the car we are riding in. She asks if, when we return from the movie and they come in for a glass of wine, the paintbrushes will be safe in the car given that our neighborhood has a history. Across the street there once lived a guy who is now incarcerated in San Quentin on Murder One. A few doors down, a group of men were busted for running a hot car ring. Every night a gang stands below the streetlight on the corner, right next to our house, young toughs who might be tempted by the looks of Joan and Nina's trunk. We talk about the odds—caution versus risk—which turns into a discussion on how the criminal mind decides who to steal from and what to steal, decides which trunks hold promise and which only a spare and a jack. In the end I say I think the brushes will be safe. I imagine the paintbrushes lying in the dark gloom of the trunk, in a wooden box lined with crushed purple velvet, like the lining you find in a saxophone case. I can see them there, snug tight in those plush sheets, resting up for their upcoming masterpiece.

Picturing the paintbrushes in repose triggers a memory, a recollection. As we ride along, I tell a story about something that happened in the house where all three of us lived so long ago, about the day my girl-friend's other girlfriend entered my bedroom, the one safe haven I had in the house, the room where no one gained entry without my say-so. It was the only place I could go when it got too weird in the halls with all the various girlfriends coming and going, in those heady days of non-monogamy. In retrospect, I feel a little embarrassed about my need for seclusion. It was as if I'd posted a sign on a tree house (or in this case my room) in large slashing letters: NO BOYS ALLOWED! But in actuality no boy, no girl, no creature was allowed entry. I was as misanthropic as the poet Robinson Jeffers on his rocky promontory, in his house made of stone on the Monterey coast, angry at the world yet still able to fashion marvelous misanthropic poems with his cranky attitude.

My room was like that stone house. There, I could think my thoughts without interruption. Often I would go there and sit at my desk with all my mementos arranged just the way I liked them: a ship's bell, the shadow box containing a heart milagro my girlfriend had given me, a fish hook, a copper flower vase I stole from a graveyard, a shard of pale violet glass, a jar full of blue-handled paintbrushes (although I did not paint, I liked the look of the brushes in the jar), a glass of water in which I submerged long tall strands of green grass collected from our overgrown back yard. The strands swayed in the water and reminded me of the sea. I loved to look at all the objects and then look out the small window next to the desk, which looked out on the back yard, the side of the brick apartment building next door where many refugee families lived, and a nice patch of sky. I would lie at night in my bed, which faced the window and the sky the window framed, and watch as clouds scudded by. The house wasn't far from the city center and the clouds overhead were backlit by the reflection of the city lights below, illuminated against the night sky in a way that would be difficult to capture on canvas. The clouds were simultaneously dark and luminous, shining light gray against the navy blue background of evening.

I was sitting at my desk one day, the desk where I didn't write, in the room where I didn't paint, thinking about the arrangement. My girlfriend's other girlfriend, my nemesis, my opponent in the game of love, was known for her creativity (she worked as a graphic designer for album covers and once told me how she had a hand in airbrushing Dolly Parton's thighs to give her a comelier shape), her agility on the soccer field, her wicked humor, her devil-may-care attitude. She was loud and boisterous and I always knew when she was around. We were all trying to be adult about the threesome but there was always competition in the air, as if our house was a soccer field and one girlfriend had to play forward and attack and one had to sit back as goalie and protect what she had. I felt mostly on the defensive, and in truth often choked on the playing field. With a clear lane to the goal, something in me would freeze and I'd take a kick but the ball would go off on a slant, wide of the net.

This other girlfriend showered my—or *our*—girlfriend with lots of gifts. She had lots of money and spread it around, yet I always felt the generosity was full of false showmanship. There was a rehearsed, Jerry Lewis-like quality about it. Behind her back I called her the Queen of Visual Philanthropy. Every other day, our girlfriend—hers and mine—was sporting something new: rip-stop running pants, an Alaskan cable knit sweater, a cute pink bicycle cap. I was working as a handyman for a group of homeless shelters, which meant driving a beat-up truck around and moving bad mattresses from one flophouse around to the other flophouses. The pay was awful, so the only thing I could give our girlfriend was not much.

I was sitting there at the desk, looking at my things, concentrating on having my own thoughts, when I heard a ruckus in the hall. My girlfriend and her other girlfriend were coming in from a soccer game. I heard their laughter, then heard the soccer ball bounce off the hallway wall, take a muffled roll on the carpet, and come to a stop near my closed door. I heard the other girlfriend shout *Goal,* which sounded faintly sexual. I heard her laugh and laugh.

I was trying to focus hard, staring intently at the heart milagro, when I heard the doorknob turn. The other girlfriend came in, just walked in, as if invited. Or as if uninvited. It didn't matter. She was in. I didn't have a lock on my door. I think she smiled but I can't be sure of that. If she did it was a wicked smile, a piss-on-you smile, an I'm-going-to-pull-your-little-chain smile. She was either wearing black running shorts and a blue, yellow, and white striped rugby top or navy blue running shorts and an orange, green, and white striped rugby top. I can't remember. She either had a red bandanna wrapped around her head or a lavender scarf tied jauntily at the neck, French style. I can't remember.

I only remember that she walked over to my desk and without saying a word grabbed all the paintbrushes in the jar, grabbed them all up in one motion that now seems rehearsed, as if she had practiced this motion over and over at home, practiced with pencils, with cooking spoons, with long-handled things, a motion full of purpose and grace. With that practiced grace, she flipped the brushes so that the bristles were pointed up, toward the sky, toward the clouds racing by, and then dropped them back into the jar. The ends of the paintbrushes made a woody *tat-tat-tat* on the bottom of the jar, so unlike the silent absence of sound when I put them in originally, in their brushes down position.

The other girlfriend didn't say anything. The gesture was instructive, catty, clear. Then she turned and walked out the door.

At first I couldn't see straight. I couldn't see period. I saw nothing in front of me, nothing out the window. All I could do was replay the scene in my mind; *her* walk, *her* entry, the flip of *her* wrist, *my* brushes twirling, the sound of the tips of the handles on the glass, *her* exit. When I regained sight I looked at my desk again, then at the brushes. I looked at the brushes with their bushy little tails pointing up, not straight up but bent a little, like sea grasses at the shoreline permanently bent towards land, slanted from a north wind coming off the ocean. I stared at them for a long while.

With one defining motion and in one moment everything about the arrangement of my mementoes changed. The desk changed, the room changed. My carefully constructed world changed. Now everything seemed out of order, purposely rearranged. I once worked at a Montessori school and hated the regimentation of it all, the fixation on putting everything in its place. I fantasized about coming in after hours and putting the wood blocks where the toy trucks belonged, taking the nap mats out of their bin and stacking them on top of the hamster cage, but I never had the guts to go through with my diabolical plan.

It wasn't her audacity, her gall, her intrusion on my private world that surprised me. That was to be expected from her. I anticipated she would do something like this, like a tactical movement on the soccer field, a fake head butt. She was just the kind of person who could make that gesture, so confidently, without stumble, so like the motto of the Green Berets: Swift, Silent, Supreme. She could pull off an affront like this and not think twice.

Then something else rose to the surface. I realized what the gesture suggested: I'd been found out. I knew nothing about painting or art, about the care of paintbrushes, hadn't realized the bristles would be damaged by my turning them upside down, brush tips hitting the bottom of the glass. They'd never be the same again, forever damaged like the time I was a passenger in the back seat of a car full of teenagers, the teenage driver, drunk as a skunk and how, speeding around a curve, he lost control and the car rolled once, twice, three times over before landing, standing up, on one side. When the car came to a stop, I was on the bottom of the heap, smashed against the car's side window with my cheek up against the glass and two people stacked up on top of me. When I moved my eyes to the left I could see the splintered glass, the pavement, could hear the small crunching sound at my shoulder when I tried to move. That's when my girlfriend's other girlfriend should have happened along and plucked me from the wrecked vehicle and in one swift fluid movement put me upright. As it was, I had to climb out myself.

⚓   ⚓   ⚓

As I recount the paintbrush story, everyone in the car laughs. I tell it with a bravado you can only have years later, after the fact, after time has gone by. I tell the story with hand gestures, pantomiming the flip of the wrist with a flair I certainly didn't possess back then. It all would be extremely funny except that my girlfriend's other girlfriend died, in fact, died recently, of cancer. My girlfriend asks if it is easier or harder to tell the story because of that. There's tension in the way she asks the question, as if I'm not honoring the dead, even though, if you think about it, I am offering up a kind of narrative memento mori. I want to explain to her that, while the other girlfriend is no longer in the world, by telling the story I've brought her back to life for a moment. A commendable act. But even as I'm offering this defense I know it's weak, what you might tell yourself when you're feeling small about how you've thought about someone, all the ill thoughts you've wished their way.

I had a dream about the other girlfriend recently. There she is, all laid out in a coffin, in her soccer clothes, the lid of the coffin opening and closing, like a door to a room or a car door, slamming over and over again, disrupting her eternal rest.

⚓   ⚓   ⚓

Reminiscence breeds reminiscence. If the storm door opens, if someone's eyes glaze over and they begin to refer to the past, others feel they have permission to go through the door as well. All of this talk triggers something in Nina and she starts to talk about Margot, her other girlfriend at the time, another girlfriend in the house, who stayed over most nights, who lived there but wasn't on the lease. Who we later learned was on all kinds of drugs: downers, coke, heroin. Maybe it started with the cross tops, the innocent-looking white tabs of speed we sometimes took before we played soccer. But it ended with heroin. Someone once told me junkies are like salmon, committed to climbing the fish ladder of drugs, a steady upward climb that starts at the sea and only ends when they reach their spawning grounds and they die. Years later, I still have a hard time saying that I lived with a heroin addict and didn't know it. To admit to being so clueless.

Both Nina and her other girlfriend worked the night shift, driving for a newspaper company, delivering bundles and bundles of freshly minted front-page news. They knew the news before anyone else and I wonder if that contributed to some sense of being out of time, as if the events of the day didn't matter. Every day something else would happen, and every day it would end up in the recycling bin. Nothing was permanent. If you already knew what was going to happen and felt you could predict people's reactions to the news—the imagined horror at the story of the ex-husband gunning down four kids in his ex-wife's home, the secret joy at a society matron exposed in a sex scandal—maybe you felt apart from others in a way.

And it's true they were solitaries. My girlfriend and I rarely saw them. They'd return from work in the early morning bleary-eyed, smelling of newsprint, and stumble off to their bedroom. The only time we saw them lucid was when they reappeared in the late afternoon to make scones in the kitchen. Every day they made scones flecked with little bits of orange rind and currants and every day they would offer us some. With this homey ritual how was I to believe there was anything untoward happening in the house—syringes and money exchanged and tourniquets and the like? Nina's other girlfriend seemed cool and brusque and sporty. And healthy. There was the Marianne Faithfull record but I ignored that sign. I have to admit I felt I couldn't read her, but at the time that didn't matter so much. In our twenties we weren't exactly looking for depth.

Ultimately, we all left that house. I won my girlfriend over time, actually in a few months, without many gifts. We moved out into an itsy apartment with one small bedroom. There weren't enough rooms in the place for spare girlfriends. My girlfriend's other girlfriend moved to San Francisco and had many, many girlfriends before she died. The soccer-scones-heroin girls followed suit and moved down to San Francisco where everything was more plentiful. After a year, the lesbian exodus swept us along, and my girlfriend and I moved to San Francisco too. There was more culture, more art, more movies and, as if to prove the point, here we are in a movie line with Nina telling us about her ex-girl-friend, the one who was on heroin, who contracted HIV years ago and, to everyone's amazement, is still living. Nina says she's seen her recently on the street, thinner, older, damaged, but still looking invincible. None of us believes it. We never thought she would live this long. We thought San Francisco was her final spawning ground.

If I were called upon to write the epitaphs for the other girlfriends' gravestones, for Nina's and for my girlfriend's ex, I would write:

> Someone who was supposed to die, didn't.
> Someone who was supposed to live, died.

⚓   ⚓   ⚓

Nina and I approach the ticket window and fumble for our wallets. I buy the ticket for my girlfriend, because now I have a good job and can treat her, can make up for all those lean years. Just before her turn to pay, Nina turns to me, hands deep in her jacket pockets, with a look on her face that means trouble. I know it has to do with the junkie girlfriend.

"You know," she whispers, soft and low so the people behind us in line won't hear. "She took something from your room once."

She says this sheepishly, like you would admit a dark secret, one you've been holding on to. As if she is still culpable, as if, by association, she had a hand in it. I quickly tell her I have long since forgotten that house and what went on there.

Other than the paintbrush story. Other than the scones. Other than the spare newspapers in the hall.

Yet now I remembered everything even more clearly. The room, the mementos, the beige carpet, the windowsill. The free box filled with our used clothes—some old bellbottoms, some worn soccer togs—that we put outside for the refugees next door. The yellow couch we found on the street that had no legs, which we carted back to the house and worked fine, except for the fact that when you sat in it your knees ended up higher than your shoulders. The time we had a Thanksgiving dinner comprised of enchiladas and beer and a few leftover scones.

She took something from your room once.

What was it? Was it worth something or only of sentimental value? Was it inconsequential or something of consequence? What haven't I carried with me all these years? What have I missed that I have forgotten?

It couldn't have been cash. I had so little at the time and I'm sure I would have noticed a dime missing from my cigar box.

I think about my desk at home, the same desk but now facing a different window. On it is the ship's bell, the shadow box, a different glass with long blades of grass I've gathered from our back yard. There's still the cemetery vase. There are also a few new things: a tiny plastic box that contains some drops of mercury, which, until recently, I would pour in my palm and stare at for inspiration until I was told that wasn't such a good thing to do. A white porcelain cup with a hairline crack that I can't seem to part with. A rainbow marble.

What if it meant nothing to her, was simply something her hand rested on like when our puppy rests his lips on a chair leg and before you know it the chair leg's been gnawed down, is hobbled and out of balance forever? What if it is something that once meant something to me, something I've been longing for all these years but couldn't get a fix on? What are the losses that we long for?

Maybe the loss of something small, insignificant—a blue pen, a pair of toy scissors—brings about all that comes after: ennui, the middle-aged crisis, the sense of loss so deep that you know that only something big—a personality transplant, a move abroad, years and years of therapy—will provide the solution. If you could have it back again—this small thing, this forgotten thing—would the possession of what once was lost give you an entirely new vision of how to organize your life, how to organize meaning?

I start to make a list of everything I've ever lost. First I remember a black Raleigh bicycle I loved. But it had been stolen, not lost. There was the rosewood-handled pocketknife that I used to open oysters, a baby's silver goblet I found in a thrift store that I used to drink ouzo from, one of my father's copper cufflinks. I lost an engraved signet ring my girlfriend gave me. Then the moss agate ring she gave me. Then the lapis ring with the diamond baguette, the last ring she gave me before she stopped giving me rings. I decide not only to list what I can hold or see and but also to include the intangibles: elasticity in my arms and legs, the ability to stay up all hours and go to work the next day, the desire to care what other people think about how I wear my hair. The list grows but it is only of the things I remember I've lost.

I make up my mind to create a flyer to post on telephone poles. I'll make a hundred copies and fill up the stapler. The flyer will carry no photo, just an empty box where you'd usually find the picture of the lost cat or dog and the following text:

> I've lost something.
> I don't know what it is.
> I can't describe it to you.
> If you find it please call.
> Reward.

⚓   ⚓   ⚓

Two weeks later I am sitting at my desk when Nina calls. "I just wanted to say again, I'm sorry."

And I say, "Oh, no need," and mean it because all of us did all kinds of nutty things back then. To make her feel better I tell her about the time I was eighteen and did some house-sitting for a really nice pair of elderly pacifists. When they returned from their European vacation—a vacation they'd saved and saved for—their washing machine was busted, their car wouldn't start, their garden, which they'd given me specific instructions to tend, was dried out and gone to seed. They looked at all of it in disbelief, the wreckage of house and home. As I was leaving, the man pulled me aside and with a look of unimaginable sadness asked me to answer just one question: *Are you working for the CIA?*

"She didn't need it," Nina said, returning to the story of her ex-girlfriend. "She was always taking things back then. It was more about the act of stealing, that small rush a person feels when they are being bad."

Like the boys in the neighborhood. Like the vase I stole from the graveyard. Like the ability to steal a moment in memory, a small humiliation, and recount it to a group of friends, to play it for laughs.

I ask her if she can try, just try, to remember what it was.

"I think she took a paintbrush."

I hadn't counted them. I couldn't even look at them after the other girlfriend turned them right ends up, but at the time I had too much pride to remove them from the desk. I left them there until we moved. Where they are now I couldn't say. Maybe they went into the free box. Somehow, over the years, I decided they were a reminder of false bravado, of façade. Never again could I look at them and not feel small.

But here's the thing: Nina's junkie girlfriend was also an artist. She painted a headless torso of a soccer player that still hangs in our house. What would she want with a damaged brush, a brush that was so badly slanted and could never paint complexity, could at best only be used for background?

Pinball

WE DRIVE DOWN THE COAST, MY FRIEND AND I, A FULL TANK, not like the last time when I drove this highway alone, from Bonny Doon to Half Moon Bay, the empty light on, the prayer in the throat, with each mile, make it last, make it last. And I tell him about that time, all the drama of it, and even though there is very little distance between us on the bench seat, I can see that he's in his own little world, and the story feels like it takes forever to reach him, and then, after traveling that expanse, must vault the boundary of his skin, to enter and roll around inside him, bouncing like a pinball off the similar lights in his imagination—whatever gets called up when I say the words "tank, empty, danger."

It's quiet for a few more miles and we pass fields of artichokes and rows of green things and brown furrows that match his furrowed fore-head—Where has the ball gone to now? What pocket?—and then he says to no one, to me, "I'm lonely when I pump gas." I look over and wonder how the pumps, the gas smells, the lone cashier behind the glass enclo-sure, solitary, *Bell Jar*-ed, the drawer for cash sliding toward you and slid-ing back, how it all combines. And I don't recoil or veer off the road, I keep an even foot on the pedal, we do not lurch or speed up or slow down with his revelation, so he feels he can continue.

"I always try to take someone with me, you know, on the way to a movie or a concert," and I can almost hear his *Do you mind if I stop? I'm a little low,* said so nonchalantly, an afterthought, and then no urgency as he slowly slides into the station, pulls up to the island, gets the credit card out, flips the little lever to open the gas door (is there a similar lever to open a small door into our hearts?), then pumps with airy confidence while inside the car his date for the evening fiddles with the radio dial and never knows the cost.

I don't offer any reply, for the pinball has fallen into a different groove in my mind. What was it about gas stations that made him lonely? Was it the public place of it, the smell of octane, the digital numbers noting gal-lons and cost clicking so fast now, so fast, speeding by and where oh where was his one true love? If he could feel such loneliness pumping gas, then what loneliness might there be in the world that I have never guessed at or imagined, that could happen in an instant, as quickly as one flicks the pump on, and your girlfriend calls long distance and admits to an affair, the world spins as fast, as out-of-control as the price of crude, as fast as the price dial, and nothing, no storage tank, no amount of fuel from an eighteen-wheeler with stainless steel cylinders, can fill the deep, deep tank.

Or was it the flags? There were always flags. They flew at the station entrances, trumpeting something, heralding the promise of something gay and triumphant. Or the gas island itself? If you were alone was the word "island" the trigger, as in, "If you were alone on a desert island and had one choice of companion who would you . . .?" Or now how each station has a little mini mart with smallish packages of things—enough for just one person—mini donuts, mini pads, mini sticks of cheese, mini Famous Amos, two tiny Famous Amos cookies in a small bag, Amos himself looking very diminutive on the cover, not the larger-than-life figure that he is. And he too is locked onto the confines of the package, never emancipated; never free to date Mrs. Fields.

I begin to compare our lives, my solitary post at the university, his lonely post at the hospital. As a nurse he deals with need day in and day out, each person's little plea for help, and when he leaves for the day is it all simply more than he can bear? And this past week, when I saw so many students and colleagues, this one and this one and this one, and each wanting something, not quite so simple as a gallon of gas, when the colleague with the angry need came in the office and I chicken-necked and said *Yes, yes, yes,* and after he left the room, said *Please get the fuck out of my life*—had it all only served to make me lonelier?

Lately I've begun to see it in other people, to be drawn to it, attracted to it, this sense of loneliness. I can picture my single friends alone in their neat apartments, their neat yellow kitchens, now the cups lined up on the shelf, all handles pointed in the same direction, the coffee pot clean and ready to go for morning, with just the right amount of grounds measured out for the single perfect cup. And I can picture their perfect opposites, the other type of loner, slovenly, the pizza box and beer cans and smelly things tossed about the room in the same neat order of disarray.

I'm not interested in the coupled, though I myself am coupled, and happily so. I've been with Shots twenty years, through sickness and in health and till death do us part, but even with all that togetherness, it never quite takes care of that odd feeling that comes up when you least expect it, the feeling that I am looking for something else, something essential, not in my life—a sense of being apart from, of being walled off. Doesn't my friend seek this too—a need to be walled off like the private garden he grows at home, the boxwood hedges he planted grown high to stop the neighbor's stare?

Everywhere I look I see them, the unattached, and everywhere I see their purposeful efforts to appear nonchalant, not wanting. I have yet to find someone who does not claim they want a match, a mate, a do-or-die partner in crime, yet often they stay single. What could be gained from such a choice? What can they teach me; what have I already lost? Is it better to lead a solitary life, where longing gives you purpose? Or better to have someone along for the ride. Someone to say: *Look there. Look there.*

Stripping

GIVEN THAT THE NEIGHBORHOOD—MARGINAL, DOWN IN THE heels, iron bars on the windows—was knee deep into gentrification, and that the houses—built in the 1950s, first bought by veterans returning from World War II on the FHA plan for fifty dollars down—Cape Cods they called them, cracker boxes we called them—had steep pitched roofs and enough attic space to create tiny rooms for the little crackers coming along. Given that these same houses, with new slap-dash paint jobs, were being placed on the market overnight, changing from rental to owner-occupied, and now the removal of the iron bars, and now the delivery of new sod, large green jelly rolls that rolled out like a plush green carpet. Given that this neighborhood—which sat high on a hill, with a stunning 180-degree view of the Pacific ocean—was known as the poor side of town (a reversal of fortune, for aren't the rich always high up on the bluffs, as in "better than," as in "a cut above?") it wasn't unusual to see a scruffy old man, one of the last original homeowners, on his daily walk, carrying an old, small, equally scruffy white-haired dog in his arms.

Every day, as I drove past on my way to work, he would leave his tumbledown house at the end of the block and shuffle up and down the sidewalk with the dog. I never really saw him, in the way that the familiar becomes invisible. He was as much a part of the landscape as were the cypress trees that grew on the bluff, or the Our Lady of Guadalupe statue that blinked off and on in the window of the house kitty-corner to his, or the fake Tuscan fountain on our next-door neighbor's front lawn. One week clear water dribbled through the fountain's sad faux spout. The next week, the water dribbled green—in a miraculous conversion and with the aid of food coloring.

Only when the old man failed to appear did Shots and I take notice. Only then did we perk up and wonder aloud what became of him and his small dog. We assumed the man had died. His house, with its dirty stucco walls riddled with cracks, looked empty. But it had always looked abandoned, as he and the dog looked, as if life or his family or the world had passed them by. Were it not for their daily walks I would have assumed the house had been unoccupied for years. I never saw evidence that lives were being lived inside those stucco walls.

That is, until the walls came down. A month after he'd gone missing, a large green truck pulled up in front of the house, on its side, in crude lettering: WE HAUL ANYTHING. A work crew tumbled out and took sledgehammers to the place. In two days, the stucco was gone, the house stripped of its outer layer. Whoever bought the place—most likely some up-and-comer with lots of cash—was going to tear it down and build something new, probably a Monster home.

Now, any passerby could see straight into the rooms, see that nothing hung from the two hangers in the bedroom's empty closet, not the old man's gray windbreaker, nor his brown polyester pants. Instead, an old guitar leaned against the closet wall, like the image you'd see on an old album cover for Segovia or Jobim. All you needed was a wine bottle with candle wax dripping down the sides, a checkered table cloth, and a cluster of grapes to complete the tableau.

Week after week the guitar sat there. No door or wall prevented anyone from coming into the empty house and taking it, which was strange given that gangs of teenaged thugs regularly roamed the sidewalk, in the slow saunter so identifiable of petit thieves, the nonchalant sloping walk that screams "we're casing the joint." I'd often see them sidle up and try the door handles on cars they passed, hoping to ransack the glove compartment or feel under the driver's seat where everyone hides things.

Ransack. Maybe the old man used that word when he talked about his family, wherever they might be. As in *When I go, they're going to ransack the place.*

The guitar finally did disappear. Maybe a young thief took it, learned classical guitar, and turned his life around. It could happen. I wasn't sure why, but I wanted the guitar to have a second life. Whatever did happen, the guitar was gone, like the old man and the dog.

The crew returned the next week and tore down all the interior walls, stripping away the plasterboard and exposing the wood framing. Now I could look straight through the house and see what I could never see. The house, positioned at the end of the street on a large corner lot, looked straight out at the Pacific Ocean. Not a tree, roof, or pole obscured a single dot of that great big blue expanse. This crummy old house had a million-dollar view, though that phrase needs to be retired or at least adjusted upward, given California real estate's skyward prices.

"It's ironic, isn't it?" I said to Shots. The old man, who looked so unkempt, who never chose to beautify his surroundings by mowing the lawn or sweeping the walk or hanging potted begonias—all the little suburban touches that say *This is my beautiful little corner of the world*—was surrounded by beauty. Extraordinary beauty. Drop-dead beauty. Inconsolable beauty. Day in, day out. Morning, noon, and night.

I pictured the old man and his dog in the kitchen at dinnertime: the man opening a can of wet dog food and putting some in the bowl, the dog wagging its stumpy little tail with whatever energy it had left. Maybe the man took the guitar out on nights like that and played something sweet and melancholy. Maybe he kept time by tapping his shoe on the dirty kitchen floor. Then both of them retired to the living room, sat on the couch facing the picture window that faced the sea, and slipped into a silent reverie to accompany the orange sunset. Maybe that's where the old man ultimately went, into his sunset. Maybe, like a married couple who have lived together for years, they both went at the same time, one dying and the other succumbing a couple days later, unable to go on.

As it turns out, I wasn't the only one to notice the new view. Every night when people drove home from work, their days spent in enclosed offices, in cubicles, without a window to open, with only taped-up pictures of Yosemite or an unpopulated beach in Martinique to take them away, they came upon the shell of the house and pulled over to the curb. Some stayed in their cars and from the driver's seat looked through the framed house and out at the ocean. Some got out and walked into the house and through the rooms—the kitchen, bathroom, bedroom that once held a man, a dog, a guitar—to see what was there to see.

I was one of those who got out and walked in. I wondered how he would have felt—an old man who never spoke to anyone, who wanted to be left alone—having me and others tramp through his rooms. I thought of him when I saw two tables inside that hadn't been carted away. One was an end table painted an awful orangey color, the paint so chipped you could see layers of other colors, years of earlier incarnations.

It was the other table that caught my eye; an oval-shaped dining table with a beveled edge around the top and carved wooden legs, possibly of the Victorian era. It was classy, a cut above. Of another time—as was the old man. The table was covered with dust and plaster and there were dirty brown smears as if someone dipped their fingers in mud and wiped them across the top. Yet beneath all this I could see a great writing table, something I desperately needed as I'd just come into possession of a writer's studio, a studio I'd dubbed the Crab Shack.

How I came into possession of the Crab Shack is another story. The short version is that I simply asked. The longer version is that one sunny Sunday I drove down the coast bent on finding a place to write, away from email, the phone, the bed to be made, the wash to be done, who knows who knocking at the front door, and all the unforeseen interruptions when you work at home. At a fishing pier in a small coastal town I asked the harbormaster if he knew of any sheds or abandoned trailers where a writer might write. He told me to walk out to the fisheries at the end of the pier and to talk to Dave, that Dave was a nice guy and he might know.

A gray two story building at the end of the dock held two fisheries, Three Captains and Morningstar. The hangar door was up on one and inside I found a tall man with a knit cap pulled low over his forehead, his hands deep in a huge tub of crab. Dave, I presumed. I introduced myself and asked if he knew of a space to write. He gave me a wary look that I knew meant he'd pegged me as one of the weekenders who come by for a little "local color," so I whipped out my credentials. My father, a commercial fisherman, had owned a fishing boat—a seventy-five-foot purse seiner, a beauty of a wooden boat built in 1934—and I'd brought the photo of the boat along. He gazed at the photo and his face softened, as if he was seeing a loved one, someone he knew, someone now long gone from the world.

Dave gestured for me to follow him up the wet stairs to his office and led me to a door at the back wall. Then, with a little ceremonial bow, he opened the door. I stepped into a big box of a room crammed with all kinds of junk: un-constructed crab boxes, an old sofa, a dirty mattress, rusty tools, ropes, a basketball, a motorcycle helmet, an ice shovel. I walked to the bank of windows at the far wall that looked out over the harbor, over the pleasure boats tied to their moorings, over the hundreds of pelicans gathered on the breakwater's rocky mounds, past the break-water out to the blue open sea. The windows were directly over the dock-ing pier where crab boats came in, hitched up, and unloaded all the crab found in the tubs below. It was a great room, a room with a view, what a view, a multi-million-dollar view, and after settling on a monthly rent Dave said I could have it. "Have at it," is what he said.

All I needed was a good writing table.

I knew I needed to strike soon. I was in a high cycle, a lucky cycle. Hadn't the Crab Shack come my way for the asking? Every night as I drove past the old man's house I thought to myself, *I could just go in and take the table,* but that didn't seem right. Who would want that kind of karma attached to a table you were going to write on?

So the next afternoon, I walked down the block and through the front door, passed the table, and found, at the back of the house, a short man with a tape measure on his belt, whistling a little tune. He looked like a man who worked for himself. He looked like a contractor.

I held my hand out as if I was the neighborhood welcome committee and had a loaf of banana bread I wanted to give him. I told him I lived down the block and asked whether he'd be willing to sell the little table I'd seen inside, the table that right now was covered with his contractor blueprints.

He smiled and gave a little laugh. "Hey sure, why the hell not? You can have the table." He probably thought it was funny someone would want the dirty old thing.

I couldn't believe my luck. I also couldn't believe I was going to get it for nothing. It didn't seem fair to the memory of the old man so I said, "No, here, let me give you something for it, how about a twenty?" I was low-balling him, but then again the table was probably going to end up on the scrap heap. I insisted. I took the money out of my wallet and waved it like a green flag.

He took the bill from my hand, slipped it in his back pocket, and said, "Okay, I'll give the money to my daughter."

We walked back into the house, over to the table. A table about to get a second life.

Maybe this was the first time he ever really took a good look at the thing. When someone else wants what you have, that's when you begin to appreciate it. Until then, it's just an old table you put things on and don't think another thing about. Maybe now, it began to look like a really old table, as in possibly antique and worth something, and given the tall tales of *Antiques Road Show*—the Stradivarius in the attic, a Picasso sketch used as backing for an old print—who knew what it might bring on the open market?

He cleared off his blueprints. He squinted at the table. He stepped back and gave it an appraising eye. "You know, I bet there was once another table leaf that made the top wider," he said. I thought I detected a new, slightly British accent.

We both bent down to look under the table. Lo and behold, there was a leaf, resting on a hidden lower shelf.

"Hey," he said, and with his contractor hands pulled the two sections of the table top apart. The top opened, parted, and the leaf underneath jackknifed, doubled in length, and created a new middle leaf. Now it was a larger, even grander old table.

"What a great writing table this will make," I said. Quickly. I saw the gleam in his eyes. I knew he was having second thoughts. But a deal is a deal, the twenty was in his pocket, and sadly, wistfully—as if he were the old man and this was his table, a table he'd written love notes on when he was young, the last mortgage payment when he was older—the contractor lifted the table into his truck and drove it to my house just down the street.

⚓   ⚓   ⚓

Shots offered to refinish the table top. I went to the hardware store and bought what she needed—a gallon of wood stripper, rubber gloves, a scraper, and wax—so the spring action on the table leaves would work. The total came to over twenty-five dollars but even with the other twenty I paid, under fifty bucks was a steal. She spent the evening stripping the top, again and again. We watched the layers vanish: first the brownish smears, the dirt, then a layer of cream paint, then a layer of yellow, each layer an era appearing, then disappearing to make way for the next. After hours of work we could begin to see down to the wood and make a guess. Walnut, maybe. Or oak.

We put the table in her station wagon, drove down the coast to the pier, hefted it up the flight of stairs to my new room, and put it under the window with the view. You've never seen anything look so perfect. I placed a radio on top, a lamp with a little green shade, a tablet of paper and a pen positioned just so, at the ready. I knew this table would bring me even greater luck. Maybe some of what the old man had learned about life while sitting at that table and gazing out at the view would seep into my stories. Maybe, via the table, he had something to tell me.

A week later, as I was getting ready to head down to Crab Shack, there was a knock at the front door. I opened it and there was the contractor, dressed in the same flannel shirt, the heavy boots, the measuring tape fixed to his belt ready to measure something. He looked way too smiley. I knew immediately this wasn't a courtesy call.

"Remember me?" he asked, and something in the way he was standing, shifting nervously from foot to foot, told me I should lie and say no. "Well, listen. I hate to tell you this . . . but the lady wants the table back."

I knew what lady he was referring to. Two weeks ago I'd seen a woman outside the old man's old house, on a day the crew was nowhere to be found. She was talking on her cell phone, pacing back and forth. Agitated. She was standing by a big SUV with license a plate that read YEE HAW, dressed in pricey weekend wear: "antiqued" stone-washed jeans tucked into pink suede half-boots. I knew she was the one who'd bought the place, maybe right after the man died. She'd paced back and forth like an owner. Like an owner who was pissed that there wasn't more progress on the house.

"But the table was out there, in the open, for the taking. For months." I said. As was the other end table. As was the guitar. "Anyone could have taken it. We slaved over it for days. We spent hours sanding and stripping—" That was an embellishment, the *we* part. Shots did all the work. I rattled off every stripping product I spent money on, at a slightly inflated cost. I added in the lemon oil I intended to buy.

"She wants it back."

"It's way down the coast." Hell if I was going to tell him exactly where.

"Listen," he said, "there's nothing I can do." He lifted his hands up as if this were a stickup or to show me that he was helpless, that his pockets were empty. I knew they weren't. My twenty was sitting in one of them. He asked for my phone number; I gave it to him, saying I needed to think it over.

Later, I kept thinking about him standing there, nodding, saying there was nothing he could do. Couldn't he do something? Couldn't he make the case to Yee Haw? When recounting the story to Shots, a phrase he said kept coming back to me. Somewhere in the middle of our conversation he'd said, "Listen, I'm being honest with you."

"That's a red flag," Shots said. "Anytime someone says 'I'm being honest with you,' you know something's up."

A week went by. I didn't hear from him. I remembered asking him to tell Yee Haw what we'd been through. All of it. How difficult it would be to retrieve the table. How attached I was now. Maybe he had. Maybe Yee Haw had a heart. Maybe she'd had second thoughts and decided to let go of the table, a table that wasn't hers in the first place.

The following weekend, he called. The message was terse: "The lady is adamant. She wants that table." The word "adamant" stuck. It seemed a word Yee Haw would use.

What were my options? I didn't want to give the table back, but I also didn't want this guy knocking on my door again. He might be out there at any time. Already I'd started crouching down below the sight line, sneaking past the windows, like I did when I walked through the house in my underwear. As if I lived in a house without walls. Was all this worth it? I wanted my privacy back.

I decided to ask my friends for advice. I wanted help figuring out the ethics of the situation. If everyone thought I should give it back, I would. But if the group consensus was that it was mine, then it was mine. I asked what they would do.

One friend wondered if the lady really was involved at all. Was her new interest something the contractor invented as a way for him to get the table back? Why hadn't she taken it earlier? She must have walked through the house a million times when she was buying the place and seen the guitar, the tables. She could easily have hefted it in her big SUV and driven away.

"If it wasn't his table, how come he took the money?" asked another. "He realized, after the fact, just what he was giving away. My guess is he wants it back to sell it for a higher price." *Antiques Road Show* came up more than once.

"Well, my husband's from the Show Me State," said another. I forgot which state that was and didn't want to let on. She said I should call the contractor up and say, "Show me the lady who's so hot to get this table back."

One friend thought, given the YEE HAW plates, the suede boots, the agitated pacing, that the woman wanted the table not for the table itself, but just because someone else wanted it.

"If you'd gone in and taken a table that wasn't yours, could someone file a police report?" asked my most frightened friend.

The response that stung the most was from a friend who looked at me like I was a ninny and said, "It's yours now. Why didn't you just lie and say you'd sold it to someone?"

I didn't want to say I just wasn't quick enough. That it didn't seem right. That I wondered what the old man would think. Would he want me to have it, someone who never said hello, who never beeped the horn and gave a little morning wave?

⚓   ⚓   ⚓

That night I couldn't sleep. Was the table aging me in a Dorian Gray kind of way? The table looked younger—newly stripped and oiled up—while I looked older, grayer. I made a decision.

In the morning, Shots and I drove to the Crab Shack, brought the table down the stairs, put it in the wagon, drove back home. The men on the dock looked at me like I was nuts.

I called the contractor and left a pissy message on his machine. "All right. The table's outside. By our front porch. I want my twenty dollars back and if *the lady* is ethical she'll pay me for the materials." If she was really ethical, I wanted to add, she'd pony up for the labor as well.

I didn't hear back that evening. The table spent the night outside. Anybody walking by could have stolen it.

I left for work early the next morning, thinking the contractor would come get it during the day. The table was there when I returned. It spent another chilly night outside.

On the third morning there was a forecast of rain.

"Okay, enough is enough," Shots announced. "He's pulling your chain. We're bringing it inside. He can pay one hundred dollars for the goddamned table if he wants it back."

I was surprised at her fierceness. I was surprised she had a specific amount in mind. She said that given the time it had been in our possession, it was ours now. We brought the table inside, a table that had been taken up and down the street like a dog in our arms, and put it down in the middle of the kitchen.

Around dinnertime our neighbor came by and said, "There was a man sniffing around your house today. When I asked what he was doing he said he was looking for a table."

I woke up that night in a sweat. I got out of bed and went to the kitchen for a glass of water. There it was, in the middle of the kitchen floor, bathed in the moonlight shining in through the window. The table was floating in that golden light. I could have pulled up a chair and written a beautiful treatise on loss. Or ethics. Or beauty.

I knew what I'd do. I'd call his fucking bluff. I'd demand to talk to Yee Haw. And if she wasn't a ruse, I'd make sure she knew what we'd gone through.

⚓   ⚓   ⚓

"Well, I wish she'd just give up on it."

That was the contractor's reply when I called at seven-thirty the next morning.

In my firmest voice, my no-bullshit voice, my don't-fuck-with-me voice, I said, "You have her call me." And I hung up.

Ten minutes later the phone rang.

The first words out of my mouth were, "Welcome to the neighborhood." I don't know why I said that.

She said her name was Cheyenne, then began to cry. "I'm so upset."

I decided to just let her talk, like a suicide hotline.

"You see there are so few things left."

What a strange thing to say.

"My father had to go into a nursing home. He has Alzheimer's, and we don't expect him to live much longer."

It was unbelievable. The old man was Yee Haw's father? He looked like he didn't have a relation in the world. Other than his dog. She looked nothing like him, with her blonde hair and fancy clothes. Where was she all those years the stucco was cracking?

I wasn't going to cave so easily. I said that the table had been left out there, in the open house, for months. She countered by saying she was waiting for her brother to come from Wyoming with a truck, that he was going to help her take it away. I told her about all our work. She said she knew how much was involved in refinishing furniture, that she'd done quite a bit of that herself. She said she knew how much the products cost.

As she rambled on I already knew that if there was any chance in hell the old man truly was her father then, of course, of course, the table was hers. If I held on, it would be like someone not giving me back the photo of my father's boat.

I took a deep breath, and told her I wouldn't keep the table.

But I didn't want to see it being taken away. I lied. I told her I'd be gone. I said I'd put it outside and that she could put the money to reimburse us in the mail slot. Somehow, all this reminded me of when Shots and I went to pick up our dog from the breeder, when he was a little white-haired pup. At the last moment, the breeder held onto his little body and cried and cried. She wanted the dog to go to a good home but she couldn't bear to part with him. They'd already been through so much together.

And there was this, another reason I didn't want to part with the table: what if this was the end of that cycle of good fortune? What if my luck went with it?

After I hung up, I realized I hadn't asked about the old man's little dog. I dragged the table outside and waited.

A half-hour later I heard her car come up. I bent down under the windowsill, and caught sight of her putting the table into her SUV. Well, only the lower half of her body. Actually, I only saw the boots. She didn't seem to have a problem hefting the thing. She didn't need a brother. After she took off I went outside, put my hand in the mail slot, and fished out an envelope. Scrawled on the front she'd written: "Thanks for giving me back my table."

My table. That galled me a little.

Inside the envelope was a twenty-dollar bill. And a five. For our trouble.

I made myself a cup of tea, then sat down at the kitchen table to think things through.

If I strip away my assumptions about Yee Haw, strip away my assumptions about the type of person who would wear boots like that, strip away the years of the old man, see him at forty, at thirty, at twenty, what would I find? If you strip away the layers, the various rationales— who deserves what, why possession is ninety-nine percent of the law— does that get us any closer to understanding another person's life, their rituals, what the old man thought about as he sat at the table in his kitchen, what he said to the dog, who Yee Haw was to her father, who the contractor might be to me? Given that I never waved, given that a table is a table is a table. Given that privacy is a thing of the past—as is ethics or honesty or doing a good turn for your neighbor. Given that we are all living in glass houses. Given all of this, do I deserve the table? Does Yee Haw? Do any of us?

I put the envelope on the kitchen table, called Shots at work, and read her what Yee Haw wrote. Then I said, "That money's for you. You did all the work. All that stripping. It's yours."

It was a relief, really. No one banging on the door. No sleepless nights.

I found another table at a garage sale, a cheap round laminated one. A Motel 6 type of table no one would bother stealing. I covered it with a green tablecloth and brought it down to Crab Shack. It would do. This table was so cheesy no one would ever take it.

A week later I asked Shots how she treated herself with Yee Haw's money. I wanted to think something good came of the whole affair.

"I'm still waiting for you to give it to me," she said.

"What do you mean? The money was in the envelope I left on the table."

"I thought that was just a used envelope from a bill. I tossed it in the trash."

The garbage had already been picked up for the week. Now we were left with nothing. But who knows what happens when things we've once owned leave our hands? Maybe the envelope blew out of the garbage truck, caught a tailwind. Maybe someone picked it up off some sidewalk and on that day their luck changed.

Kith and Kin

IT WAS LATE AFTERNOON WHEN I LEFT WORK THAT DAY, around four-thirty or five, late enough to notice traffic was picking up. The stream of cars racing past seemed urgent in their rush toward home. Nineteenth and Holloway, the main crosswalk to San Francisco State University, is known as the most dangerous crosswalk in the city—many cars have crashed and burned, pedestrians have been hit, here, at the gates of academe, this collision zone of life and higher learning. During the early part of the day, whenever a class is about to start, there is always a dash across this crosswalk by the latecomers, who have to hear one last love song in the car turned up full blast: a mad dash, for each person still hears a tardy bell ringing; forever it rings inside—some eternal tinnitus—and each person carries the memory of some teacher's harsh reproach that quickens the step just a bit.

But here, in the late afternoon, as the car traffic picked up the human traffic slowed, so much so that when it was time to cross you could make out the individuals and consider who was crossing, give each person a story, a slim narrative, could name them or their majors, imagine who waited at home and what they'd make for dinner, burritos or borscht or a little microwaveable carton of gruel.

The light was coming in from the west, from the sea that was beyond the college. The light was angled in such a way that it's possible there was a luminosity factor at work, perhaps the rods and cones of the eyes were affected. Maybe there was a scientific explanation for the beauty of the light. The sunlight seemed to separate into distinct particles ("this little light of mine") as the people became distinct ("I'm gonna let it shine") and each person had the glow of one candle's intensity.

I tried not to attach too much meaning to what I was witnessing. Shots said that's what schizophrenics do, attach meaning to random events—this, after I told her that while driving home the other night a dove kamikazied downward from a telephone wire, fell right into the road in front of my car and that my intuitive feeling was that it might suggest something coming. War or pestilence or the big shebang. Maybe I was lost in this—you can get lost in certain types of light—so when the green pedestrian light said WALK I waited and watched and that's when I first saw them coming towards me.

He was an older man, tall and stately looking, and had a posture that suggested that he had never been broken, even though by his being black I could safely assume that, given this society, there were those who had wanted to break him, those who had wanted to keep him down, hunched or somehow lower than. And if it was in response to this pressure or that he walked with a book on his head all through his childhood, I couldn't know, but he stood straight and tall and I have never seen anyone who so epitomized that description.

And she, for there was a she beside him, also stood straight and tall and, though her story must have been different from his—how could it not be?—the result was the same. They left the curb together in a way that made it apparent that they were a pair, an almost imperceptible leaning toward each other that said *We are together in this world,* and they began to make their way across the crosswalk. I passed by them and felt something that I cannot accurately express—something that felt like the warmth from a lamp on dreary day—and I was so moved by this feeling that once past I turned in the middle of the crosswalk and watched them continue to move toward the campus. It was then I noticed that the heels of his shoes were worn down, needing a cleat or resole, and that her coat—a camel plaid Burberry—was not new. There was fray at the cuffs. But they walked with such—what word could describe it? The closest word might be "dignity" or "nobility" but only if we could redefine that word, could snatch the word away from its aristocratic roots and associations, the pictures of ermine and the crown and the peerage that immediately pop up, and make grace a necessary component of the world, some part of the word's etymology.

As they moved into the crosswalk I watched students coming toward them, toward me, with the light as it was, and each person stopped in their personal reverie, stopped in their downward gaze at the asphalt, caught up in the latest test or slight, and turned to face the couple and smiled. They did not know the couple, for they did not offer a salutation or a greeting of familiarity or call either by name. But it was as if each was turning toward some fond memory, just surfacing, for they turned their faces toward the couple and smiled, beamed as a beam of light from an incoming boat casts a light on the water and was it the light or the couple's posture or the traffic or so many things that made me understand that I was in the presence of, if not one God, then at least I was in the presence of two, that all of us were in the presence of luminaries.

Was I forcing meaning? Was this making sense? For it did make sense, that here at Nineteenth and Holloway could be the site of an urban miracle, that this crosswalk might be some kind of holy ground, for many had died here, the most dangerous crosswalk in the city, so many souls had risen from this very spot, this asphalt. Maybe there was an explanation, maybe the souls never flew away. Maybe they lingered to gather here and by their presence created some film or prism (was there a combination of scientific and metaphysical explanations that doubled the moment's intensities?) and changed the particles of air, so that when the sun came in that slant afternoon light, it moved through the particles of human souls and lit the couple, the students, the traffic home. And it was this light that was like the light of the people I recalled from the past, loved ones now long gone from this world.

Maybe someday I would find all the missing ones on a boat sailing around a harbor. Relatives who had long since passed on—my two Nanas, the baby lost on the passage over from the old country, the grandfather in the mine, the father gone to sea. And there, too, on the boat might be my modern kith and kin, the young men lost to the virus and the women who had left the earth without breasts and the little girls in ditches and so many more. They would all have on little party hats and Japanese lanterns—luminescent, in every color, red and yellow and green—would hang from the netting. The boat's hold would hold ice and every kind of drink and someone would yell *Down the hatch!* and down there, in the hatch, would be every lost thing, every lost feeling, every lost hope, and all we desire that is forever gone from this world. And that's where manners went and dignity, and that's where one would never feel lonely, not for a moment and here now, here we are at the dock, hop on board and never lonely again.

Pink Harvest

SHE STANDS AT THE KITCHEN WINDOW, FILLETS THE SALMON, slices a straight line down the belly of the fish. She could do this in her sleep. Outside, the sky is full of red clouds, the kind that appear only in winter. Red sky in the morning, sailor take warning. Red sky at night, sailor's delight. Since it's afternoon she breathes a sigh of relief.

The front door opens. He comes in, plants a kiss, longer than usual, then throws a fat package on the drain board. She picks up the package to weigh it, her hands accurate scales, figures she's dealing with three pounds of something. Without further ceremony tosses off the newsprint. Inside a mound of pure pink fans out, the color so vivid it takes a moment for her eyes to adjust. She looks closer. The shrimp become distinct, individual. Some lie hooked together, entwined, a baby's finger curled around the mother's. Take a good look, he says. Pink harvest of the sea.

He starts in, tries to sell her on a new gamble. As if her whole life with him isn't one. Someone has gotten hold of his ear, convinced him of money to be earned fishing shrimp instead of salmon, the salmon he has spent a lifetime tracking. He reaches down, scoops some up, the shrimp dripping through his fingers. He believes in the possibility of a big return, can picture his hands plowing through piles of money, green bills floating through the air. She notices how small the shrimp are. So pink. So feminine. How they drift down like petals. How can he risk their economic future on something so delicate?

He asks her to look at this a different way. He tells her to let her eyes drift, adjust her sights downward. He tells her the bottom of the sea is pink.

He will illustrate his point. Outside the kitchen window, the sky is red. The sea will be calm tomorrow, something she knows to be true. He builds on that, predicts a glowing future, says the sky is a reflection—not of the sunset but of what lies below the waves.

There is no hindsight at the start of a journey, no indication of outcome. All we have is what we can conjure. She turns back to the cutting board, tries to think: how the color of the sky can influence the water, how the bottom of the ocean can influence the sky.

The Prize Inside

GET A FISH, SNAPPER OR LINGCOD, MACKEREL OR HALIBUT, AN everyday fish, a regular fish, not a special fish, not albacore or swordfish or salmon—too fancy for this common dish. Put the fish in a soup pot, cover with water, let it come to a slow boil, like your mother's slow boil as she waits for your father's fishing boat to come in, for his ship to come in, for him to make good on his promise to fix the leaky gutters this time he's in port. Cook until the juices of the fish are released, then simmer. The simmering goes on for minutes or hours or days, for weeks or months or years, fish is simmering on the stove forever, from cradle to grave, the fish simmers and simmers and at some point is done.

Lift the fish out to place it on a platter. As you lift, the meat falls away from the bones, millions of bones, the ribs, the spine, the long bones, the short, the flat bones, the small bones around the cheeks, like lacework, the intricate system of delicate, delicate bones, and now the need to pray to Saint Blaise, patron saint of things caught down the wrong pipe, and now the need to go to church and have the priest draw two white candles across your neck and bless your throat, so the bones won't get caught and choke you to death. And once blessed, *tell me*, your mother will say, *how can you swear like you do, like your father swears, how can you say jebem— fuck—so easily that foul language rolls off your tongue?*

What remains in the pot is fish stock, golden broth, that can cure all, a sore throat, a sore life: a salty cure. Now add potatoes, cubed, or rice and peas like the Italians, reeezi beeezi, that's what you say, and simmer until the rice is cooked and puffed up, and the air smells salt sweet, perfumed by the sea.

Place the platter on the dinner table, on display. You listen, with your sisters on either side, while your father talks about the other Slavs, about the lack of money, lack of fish, about who is getting screwed, jebem, jebem, jebem. Hear your mother slip in something about the weather, the forecast for rain, the gutter. See your father gaze out the window at the horizon, just outside, calling him, though he's only been in port one day. Today in school you learned about Christopher Columbus. Did he too have the same look standing at the helm, on the lookout for the New World? You play around with what's left of your meal—why does it take them so long to eat?—and *Finish everything on your plate,* she'll say, and then you sit. And then you wait.

On the platter all that is left are the bones, the backbone like the one you see in the cartoons, where the cartoon cat tips over the trash can in the alley and pulls out the fish spine, with only the head and tail intact. Here there's no escaping the face, the open mouth, the eye looking upward, toward heaven or the ceiling light, it was living and now it's dead, and you focus in on the white eye, like the pupil-less eyes of the zombies you saw in the science fiction film *The Night of the Living Dead,* zombies who looked just like regular townspeople the day before—the mailman, the neighbor, the school nurse—then the next day were walking with their arms stretched out in front of them, coming to claim you, coming your way. You look at the eye, covet it, think to yourself, it's not a crime, what's about to happen next: the fish no longer uses its eyes to evade the net, the hook, to see whatever it is a fish sees. The fish is blind to what will happen next, the soul already gone, as we are blind to what will happen, tomorrow, the next day and the next, blind to what lies just around the bend.

And now begins the arguing, the fight every time, who gets the prize and who got it last, and *You always get your way* and *You're a lying cheat,* for the fish has only two eyes and there are three daughters and someone will be left out. Someone always gets left out.

But tonight I'm the lucky one. Tonight, I get an eye.

When I put the eye in my mouth it tastes salty and fishy and good, and when I chew it's a little chalky. (*Remember,* she says, *don't tell your friends at school about the eyes.*) I chew and chew, it's not the taste I covet, it's the prize inside the eye, inside where we cannot see. When the white is gone, there it is, the clear round center as tiny as a small glass bead. If you hold it up and look closely it's like looking inside a clear globe and there you'll find a sea and sky, and there, I spy a boat and there, a sea full of fish, and in this world the sea is always calm and the sky is always clear, and if I could vault this life, into the world inside the eye, my vision would expand, I could see into the future: I could see beyond the kitchen table, beyond the house, to the world past this life.

And what's that out there, Captain, just around the bend? And what's that out there, Christopher Columbus, just beyond the horizon's edge?

The Nickel

THE NIGHT BEFORE, IN BED, I DRAW UP THE COVERS AND MAKE A PLAN.

I'll wake up with a toothache, stick my tongue in the side of my cheek. "There was blood on the pillow," I'll tell my mother, "bright red blood, a pool of it, no, it's gone now, I already washed it off, but there was lots of it, with little clots like bits of pudding. No, the dentist will make me put on pig nose, the thing he straps over my face. He'll smile, and say "Breathe in," and I'll hold my breath as long as I can, but then I'll see the kewpie doll floating above my head, its pointy head and squinty eyes, and the next thing I wake up in a dark room spitting blood into a basin that looks like a silver kidney."

I'll double over and say, "It hurts, the pain is shooting from here to here, on the left side, on the right side too, no, it's nothing I ate, it's all over, and hot, yes, feel my forehead, I'm burning up, I was a second ago, maybe the chills cooled me down. I feel dizzy. If I have to get up and walk to the kitchen I'll stumble and hit my head and bleed on the toast."

If she lets me stay home I'll promise to be as quiet as a mouse, a cat, a dove. I'll read my favorite book, *The Trail of the Sand Hill Stag*, and when I finish I'll tell her the story, all about a boy who couldn't shoot a deer. He spent day after day hunting him down, "tracking the mighty buck," in a snowy forest and when he finally finds him, deep in the woods, he looks straight into the deer's eyes and can't pull the trigger. I'll quote her my favorite line: "Bright, unsad failures they."

And my mother, who is lonely, will sometimes let me stay.

If I don't convince her that I'll die if I have to go, then the bus will come and it will start up as soon as I climb on board. Where should I sit, in the front so I can yell, "Please stop, please stop, let me off," though the driver won't listen, he never does, he'll just shout, "Sit down!"

Or should I sit in the back where I can hunker down low in the seat, I wish Daryl Erickson would stop staring at me, like there's something up my nose, *See something green, Daryl?* and I'll have to pee but I'll have to hold it, because everyone knows what happened to Nancy Olsen, who peed in her pants last year and now no one comes near her except to tag her at recess and run and yell, "Nancy Olsen's germs, no returns."

That's what my life will be, like Nancy's, a sad, sad failure, if my mother makes me go.

If I win her over she'll say, okay. This one last time. But when my father returns from the sea there'll be no excuses, no arguments. When he's in port he'll drive me to school.

⚓   ⚓   ⚓

"Open your hand," he says. He's hiding something behind his back, some bribe. I put out my palm and he drops something round and cold inside. I open my hand and see the nickel. Then he says, "If I had a million I'd give you half."

I look at the nickel, feel the weight of it in my palm, wonder how the coin will save me, turn it over a couple times, study one side, then the other. On the tails side there's a building with stairs and columns and a domed top that looks like a big bald head. The building floats in the silver air and if I could I'd walk up the steps, slide between the columns, go through the front door, find a secret hallway or a secret place under the stairs, an alcove, a broom closet, I would disappear inside Monticello and no one would ever find me again.

On the heads side is a man with a tall square collar and a ponytail. Jefferson or Washington or Adams. If I wasn't missing so much school I'd know who he is. He's staring at the words "In God We Trust" floating on the rim, but there's one word he can't see, there behind his head, "Liberty." I want liberty, which means the freedom to never go to school, where I'll have to pee, where I won't be able to hold it. The man has a pony tail and so do I but I'd bet this nickel he doesn't know how to use Alberto VO5 to slick back the sides and keep the stray hairs in.

"Hold it tight," my father says, and I hold the nickel tight enough to tattoo IN GOD WE TRUST onto my skin. For protection. I flip it over and press in the other side too. E PLURIBUS UNUM. What does that mean? My teacher would say, "Sound it out and you'll get a clue." *E plur-i-bus-u-num.* Pluribus. A plural bus. I have to ride with the others. Not a single bus of my own. A plural bus. A plural bus that makes you numb.

I climb up into the Jeep. He pulls out the choke, then pumps the pedal and turns the key. The engine coughs like a sick old man and won't turn over. It's damp and cold and the heater's busted, so I hold my hands up to the lights on the dash and pretend the golden dials are warm little suns. I check the gas gauge, see the red arrow on empty, past the E; it always is. Will we run out? Doesn't he ever check?

The engine coughs again, then starts up, he smiles, he knew it would, and now we're moving, but the sooner we get going the sooner we'll get there and he'll leave me on the steps and I'll have to walk into the school building with its wet hallways, its wet classrooms, with the maps of the world dripping over the radiators, onto the desks, dripping onto the floor. I'll hang my raincoat on a peg in the cloakroom with the other coats, hanging there like limp ghosts or bats, ready to come to life when you least expect it and fly into your hair and the day will go on and on, the day will drip and drip and drip. Will he be there when I get home or already be gone, off to sea, sailing off the map of the world? We're going fast now, too fast, speeding downhill. He pumps the brakes, nothing happens. He pumps again, no dice. He laughs and pumps, finally they catch, and the Jeep fishtails left, then right, and almost slides off the road.

The clouds are heavy and low, we drive under them, like driving under a low bridge, and he says, "You better duck your head." The sky's a gigantic gray sack full of water about to burst. We drive the long way, around Forest Park, the evergreens like dark curtains that are hiding something in back, in the dark hallways of the forest, where I'm not to go, she's said that a million times, where bums are huddled over a fire heating up their cans of beans, just waiting for a girl like me to come along, to jump on. I tell him I can see the smoke from their campfires and he says, "Bullshit, that's just low-lying fog," and I know I need to make a plan, quick, and I say, "Please go slower, please turn around, let's go to the docks, I'll help with the nets." But he says he has something he wants to show me, he promises it'll be good, and I believe him because even though he never has a million, he doesn't lie, and so we turn another bend.

The rain begins to spit and ricochet off the top of the Jeep, off the hood, then someone turns the faucet on full blast. The windshield wipers swipe away an ocean and another ocean takes its place so he turns on the headlights, which shine on each drop in the silver air. I try to count as many as I can, tell him to slow down so I can get an accurate count, and now we go around another bend, past the stone walls covered with green velvet moss, past the pond full of skunk cabbage, past the bear cage with the two sad bears hibernating inside the cement cave, and *C'mon, let's go around the park again,* go over it again, repetition, my teacher always says when I fail, when I rush with my cursive, you're missing something, go over the letter again, make the two curves of the capital E.

Then there's a flash.

To the left, under the boughs. Like lightning. There. In the space between the grass and low boughs. Like a tear in the curtains. White, bright light. Underneath the boughs.

He pulls over to the side of the road and cuts the motor.

There are six, seven, moving together against the dark green. White deer. Bright white. They glow. Neither of us says a word. Where did they come from? They do not startle and run away. Their tails twitch now and then, a flick of light. Slowly, they lower their slender necks to pull at the blades of grass and when they bend down the light curves and stays and does not disappear, soft white curves, the best cursive and no one around to wash the board clean.

A buck lifts his head, signals to the others to be on alert, for the shot, the footfall. A doe raises her head, stares my way. She has coal-black eyes and I try to give her a sign, a nod. I look into her eyes to let her know there's nothing to fear, it will be all right, and I think I see her nod back, I swear she does, and everything else drops away, the rain, the trees, the road, the sky. I look over at him and he's staring too and I want to whisper something, something like *We are here, we are here,* but I don't. There's nothing else around the bend, this is what was around the bend, if you go far enough, if you have someone to show you, and I am not frightened, of the dentist or Daryl or the kewpie doll, because if there is this, if around the bend are white deer, if there are nickels and he will ferry me, the bus will disappear, the school, the damp rooms, the radiator's hiss. When we start up again I know I will still see them, the curved light, deer not bound by rules, no attendance, no raising of the hand to go pee, no boat in the storm, no death waiting for him on the high seas, they are here always, and if not here somewhere else, if not here, around another bend. In heaven or somewhere off the map.

And he doesn't say anything. He just looks over and smiles.

He pulls out the choke, turns the key, and this time it starts up, no problem. We drive the rest of the way in silence. The rain starts up again, each drop a silver coin raining down, the sky is full of coins, we've hit the jackpot. "We're rich," he says softly, as we speed along. *We're rich.*

He pulls the Jeep up to the entrance of the school. I reach for the door handle. "Give 'em hell," he says when I jump out.

I walk up the steps, flip the nickel in the air, watch the silver spin. It comes up heads—Liberty—and I walk through the school columns and don't turn back to wave.

Digging

We either forgive each other who we really are
or not
—"Love's That Simple," Ralph Angel

MY MOTHER AND I SIT ON THE SOFA IN HER TINY APARTMENT in Everett, my city of origin, a small town in the great Northwest. Well, maybe less great than it used to be, as are these digs she's lived in since my father died on the fishing boat and took the big house and the dreams with him. We are watching the evening news, an activity we slip into happily, something to fill the air, even though it's the first night I'm back home for a visit and we shouldn't have already run out of things to say. There is fighting in Sarajevo, in the former Yugoslavia, our land of origin. Her parents grew up on the Dalmatian coast and left family and friends behind to give it a shot in America. So, it's a country that's once removed for her, twice removed for me. It's all in how you measure distance.

On the TV, an anchorman leads a camera crew down into a church basement that currently serves as a makeshift hospital. The worn faces peering back at the camera look eerily familiar. One old man on a cot, around seventy, about the same age as my mother, has a bandage sashed around his chest. He is the spitting image of my Uncle Ivo—the same nose, ears that radar out of his head. But Ivo got out long ago, made it to the new country during Tito's reign, when you could still leave. My mother always said Ivo got out while the getting was good.

The reporter addresses the people in Serbo-Croatian and, before the BBC voice dubs over, for a few small seconds, I can comprehend a word here and there. I can make out "nishta," which I know means "nothing." Maybe the question the reporter is asking is, what do you have now? *Nishta.* What do you hope for? *Nishta.* What does the future hold? *Nishta, nishta.*

The English translation kicks in. A man who lost his left arm in a bomb blast tells the reporter that the rest of his family is gone. When asked if he would now take refuge in another country, he says, "Why would I want to leave everything I have?" He spreads his good right arm wide to the horizon, as if to make a comment, to underscore. The camera pans a countryside pockmarked with mortared homes and bombed-out farmhouses. His eyes are shining with some weird belief, like a stage mother, like the parent who looks at her homely female child, lumpy and lopsided, and sees a future beauty queen.

The picture shifts to a hillside with columns of gray smoke. There's a popping sound of gunfire, then one blast, then another. My mother looks up from her knitting—green and blue checkerboard slippers for the homeless shelter—shakes her head, then returns to her task.

Usually, we don't touch it, this present past, how what's happening right now in the old country figures into our current lives. She never volunteers an opinion about the war—as if it's too revealing, as if she were telling a stranger some shameful intimacy. Maybe if you want to leave the past—the accent, the foreignness—and stamp your children American, then it's best to never refer back. You can only address the old country in sentimental moments, at the end of the meal, when you're with your kind, when gush is forgiven.

There they are, my kind, on the coffee table, assembled in a jumble of picture frames. Not an inch of tabletop shows. The frames huddle together to form a little community, as if the people inside are seeking warmth and union. There are pictures of my married sister, who lives close by—close enough to be there for my mother's health emergencies—pictures of my unmarried cousin Mate, Teta Barbara, a family picnic in a park, Uncle Ivo in front of the Dalmatian Hall. Looking at them, I remember how as a teenager all I wanted was to be anything but Slav. The blonde seventh-grade girl I had a crush on was named Marcia Darrington. I used to say her name over and over just to hear the ring of it. The name suggested neat edges, the upper crust, the final suffix, "ton," an English word no less. In our community, everyone was an "-ich." There were other differences, too: "getting an education" meant making it to secondary school; "climbing up and out" meant moving from blue to white collar, the chance to stay clean through a full day of work.

Since I moved—to get away, get educated, to live a modern life—my visits home have always been brief, quick fly-bys to maintain connection, but never long enough to ruffle. We only have so many stories to tell.When I return home to visit with my multisyllabic words, my educated gift of gab, it's as if I've forgotten our common language, the way the voices at the dinner table rise and fall, the song of it. Maybe, too, I've forgotten a basic Slav know-how: how to fillet a fish, how to tell a good person from a jerk, how to touch people when you talk to them—on the arm, the leg—all the broad gestures, the broader emotions, how to sing.

How can I make my mother hear this, the dissonance I hear when I come home again, the test of each return? How can she ever understand who I've become?

There's footage of a Serb soldier in a trench, a cocky angle to his helmet, a guy's guy. *Rambovich.* It's all too dramatic not to note, not to take a stab at. The news reaches into the room on spindly arms, wraps around us, in our calcified positions on the couch, like those death skeletons of Käthe Kollwitz, arms that encircle us like a winter wrap. Like when you bundle up the baby a little too tight.

"What did your mother tell you about the old country?" This is how I always start. If the question registers, she's not letting on, she just continues to knit, to grow green and blue rows. I am used to her stonewalling about the past—the painful reentry into memory, poverty, troubles. I have tried to analyze her silence: Is it that making a link to the past might bring the conditions back? To remember strife is to welcome it again through the back door?

"She must have told you something."

"She didn't say. She was always pining."

"Pining" is such an old-fashioned word. A word that conjures images of fainting couches and widow's walks and shawls thrown around shoulders against the chill of the sea. Someone cold and left. The word should silence me; it should be answer enough.

"She had to mention something else." I'll risk it. It's true we are of different generations. I revel in this type of excavation. In therapy, I have always mined any nubbin of a mystery, have processed out what's hidden. But even I know what thin soup a word like "process" is, know that rumination is the luxury of those who work with their heads, not their hands. What equivalent did she and her mother have? It's hard to imagine my Nana, uneducated and silent, dressed in eternal black after her husband died, sitting beside her daughter on the couch and having a heart-to-heart.

The slippers are taking form. I try to picture the Bosnian man on TV with checkerboard feet. Better to knit a rifle sling, or an ammo belt, or a grenade pouch. Think big: Knit a bomb shelter.

She fingers the channel changer, itching to switch to *Jeopardy*, though there's a good fifteen minutes of the news left. It's not like I haven't seen this maneuver before—my mother's personal flak jacket. When I protest she says, "I watch it to keep my mind sharp." I hate having to endure a half hour of Alex Trebek, the whistles and bells when a contestant picks the Daily Double, all those questions about art and politics and history. I want to shake my mother awake, tell her: Here's the real news. Here's history. Look at these people. Here's the real Double Fucking Jeopardy.

She gives me a look with a sting to it, the same look she gave me the time I called my boss an asshole. She tried to be sympathetic—any family member against the world—but then volleyed her hardest stone: "Life's not fair." Then, peering at me out of the corner of her eye, "What made you so hard?"

⚓   ⚓   ⚓

The picture on the news is of a kid with no legs. Let's talk fair. How much time is left? What happens if everyone goes, what happens if they all drain out? Already the Serbs have bombed Vukovar, Dubrovnik. With every bomb a piece disappears. And the relatives who made it here, who hold it all—memory, history—like money stuffed in a coffee can and buried in the back yard? Her older brothers and sisters have gone, to cancer, to diabetes. If I tally up my mother's current list of ailments the odds aren't good: two small heart attacks in the past year, a bleeding ulcer, phlebitis in her left leg. Events I'm never present for, though she took care of her mother forever, the old country way. Each Slav house always had a spare room for the mother's eventual return, prepared with the embroidered pillowcases, the easy chair, ready for when the time came. A room I'm reminded I lack when my mother comes to visit my rent-controlled studio.

It's true, I'm not always forthcoming when she wants to be let in on my life. There's the let's-ignore-it gay thing, the lack-of-direction-when-are-you-going-to-find-a-good-job thing, the how-can-you-live-in-such-a-hovel thing. I'd rather tell her fiction and obliterate the facts. Or at least hide them. Maybe it's in both of us, when it all gets too much. The desire to rewrite a chapter—or abolish it all together.

⚓   ⚓   ⚓

Last week Shots and I invited two of our old friends to a dinner party, two women who didn't know each other but had a lot in common. Both were nurses, both worked with the poor, both were looking for meaning in their lives. The older nurse was jaded, and, in truth, had grown small-hearted through the years, while the younger one was full of belief and hope, something I yearned for. I felt the combustion would be good. You bring people together and watch the experiment.

We all had a little wine, and the older nurse, Helen, began to tell her life story. Because she and I go back a ways, I noticed she was leaving out the hard parts. A failed affair with the first woman she was involved with, the loss of beloved parent and, most importantly, a traumatic miscarriage. The younger nurse, Kate, kept prodding for personal details, which some might call interest and some would call prying. When it got close to why Helen didn't have kids, I knew it was the next question.

Helen was describing the house she lived in with her lover, their farm animals, a Bobbsey Twins world. Kate leaned close and said, "You know that kind of home life, stable, secure, you know, that's the best environment to bring up . . ."

I could see it in the air. I could see the voices meeting each other above the table, picture the little boxing trunks, the ring, see them duking it out. Some voice was going to win.

And then it happened. Kate looked at Helen's face, started, then stopped, bumbled a few incoherent words and stopped again. She turned red, then looked back down at her plate, as if it held an answer. What unspoken force did Kate meet in midair? What crash wall turned her back, stopped the potential question and caused her to lose the power of speech?

♆   ♆   ♆

There's a commercial for a two-ton pickup. Then one for antacid. Then one for a Friday evening program schedule called TGIF. Maybe I'll suggest we have a drink, an early cocktail. Sometimes that eases things.

My mother gives a little cough, some signal, shifts in the chair, then clears her throat. Then whispers something, barely audible:

"Digging."

"What?"

"Digging. Nana said there was digging."

I leap on it. "What? Potatoes, troughs?"

She picks up a new skein of yarn, magenta-colored, and starts to rewind it.

"Just digging."

It's up to me to imagine. I've seen pictures of the old country, the land mass edged by the Adriatic, too blue to look real. The rocky soil of the islands must have made it particularly rough, the shovel hitting stone. Or bone? What could you grow in such unforgiving earth?

"Anything else besides digging?"

The news anchor is reporting the Dow's hit a new high. The needles hit each other a little harder, like heels on a waxed floor, *rat-a-tat-tat*. For a minute my mother looks like her mother, as immovable. How will she forgive me my prodding? How can I forgive her silence? It's what we've been doing all our lives, our ritual. But there's something else. On down the road, how will we get back at each other? Only when Nana was in a rest home was she forced to wear the garish-colored bed-robes her daughters brought her. Payback for all those years of black.

"Fiestas. They worked hard and then they had fiestas."

Hard to imagine Nana, her black skirt swirling, as the tamburitzas played.

I remember Nana here in this country, moving around in her backyard garden. She never had much to say to me. But once, when I visited, in the midst of some deep high-school funk about the meaning of existence, she took me aside. We were both dressed in black, my nihilistic uniform, her widow's dress. We edged around the plants in silence. Here and there she'd bend over, scrape the dirt around the base of the greens or rake at the soil. Then, out of nowhere, first in Slav, then in broken English, a kind of all-purpose advice: "Malo po malo." Little by little. She said, "Go out and put your fingers in the dirt, under a plant. Move the dirt around. Malo po malo. Malo po malo. Dig, a little."

The news shifts to Rwanda, another makeshift hospital, another language. The news anchor gets on and makes his final commentary: "With time running out—in Bosnia, in Rwanda, in Azerbaijan—what will be our official answer to these hot spots around the globe? In the face of rising tensions, what will we ultimately be called upon to do?"

It doesn't seem to register. My mother gets up from the chair, puts her knitting down, gets ready to make dinner. But, as she moves past the TV, she gives a little parting shot. "Forgive faster" she says, then flicks the TV off.

Tilting

DRAGOVICH CAME DOWN THE ALLEY, BOWLEGGED, AS IF A cannonball had shot through, hair parted and combed, wearing some-one's discarded suit jacket, past its prime, as was Dragovich.

When he came to where the alley dead-ended into a back yard he stopped, found the arbor, crossed the threshold into the garden (perhaps not the only threshold crossed that day, maybe soon the bride swung up like a feather or a sack of potatoes, the door kicked in, the promise of a new life).

Jela was digging in the azaleas, pouring fish fertilizer on the plants, overpowering any sweet scent of garden—the gladiolas by the fence, the honeysuckle, the plum tree in bloom—all this no match for fish, dead and ground, a thick brown liquid that would revive the unconscious and then knock them dead again.

She looked up, saw him there, tilting in the breeze, fumbling with his jacket buttons, up to something. What did he want this time? The accordion? A jug of wine?

He spoke first. "How are you, Mrs. Mirosevich?" He used the formal greeting out of respect for her husband who had long since passed on, who had died at sea. "What are you doing this fine morning?"

"Scratching myself," she said under her breath. What does it look like, fool.

"What's that?"

"A little of this, a little of that." There was a long silence. She poured fertilizer with new resolve. He continued to tilt in the wind, his face full of spring, as if his nose were stuffed with roses.

There was a rustling, leaves or the scrape of grapevines on the trellis. He cleared his throat. "I don't mean to change the subject, but will you marry me?"

The breeze died down, and with the question, as if slapped, she revived, her sense of smell suddenly keen, as if she could smell the man who had inhabited the suit jacket before Dragovich, could remember the way her husband's scent lay on the pillow in the mornings, a mix of cigar and fish and the sea.

She stopped, weighing the proposition. "What you got?" she asked.

"I got a house."

"I got a house too."

He tilted his hat and turned to go. Bending back over a plant she heard a quick snap, looked up in time to see him pluck a pink camellia blossom off the bush, fit it into his lapel. As he moved away she was standing on the dock, eyes to the horizon, watching her husband's boat fade in the distance, as she now watched Dragovich get smaller, his walk down the alley to his house, no hesitation, sure of step. Without warning he changed course. Turning into Mrs. Vitalich's garden, he passed under a new arbor—palms open, hopeful, ready to receive.

Truant

AFTER THE FIFTH DAY OF TRUANCY, THE SCHOOLTEACHER PAID a call, even though the family had recently come from Croatia, the smell of the old country was still on them, something moldy and earthy mixed with the not-so-faint scent of decaying fish.

She got out of her car, straightened her skirt, took one last breath of fresh air as if preparing to go underwater, then walked through the front gate and down the cement walkway.

On either side of the walk were plum trees and pine, in the garden plate-sized camellias, hydrangeas as big as faces, and in one neat plot a profusion of edible greens. "Profusion"—now that's a word she shouldn't use with them. The lawn was a deep soft green, dotted with dandelions. She heard they made a sweet wine from the yellow weed, which likely robbed them of any ambition.

The older boy had already dropped out of school, a lost cause. His younger sister, a student in her class, wore the same old woman's outfit to school every day: a dark navy blue nylon dress that was badly hemmed and poorly altered to fit. The family never threw anything out. Everything was used and then reused.

She wondered about IQ. She could never get anything across to these children, as if the distances of continents, of oceans, lie between them, as if simple custom and comprehension were languages neither would learn. What did they *know*? What did they teach them back in the old country? *Were* there teachers?

⚓   ⚓   ⚓

As the schoolteacher came down the walkway, the mother was at work in the garden, dressed in a faded brown dress, old men's work boots, with a scarf tied around her head. She was bent over the earth, her hands deep in the soil. Out of the corner of her eye she watched every step the teacher took. The mother was known by all to have such second sight, such prophetic sight, such unschooled sight, that it's possible she saw the schoolteacher coming from miles away: saw her gather her books, leave the school, get into her car, check the gas gauge, make a mental note to fill up, then drive across town, across the tracks, from nice neighborhood to this house that sat right on the railroad tracks, only an alley between the back door and the engine's blow. The mother may even have possessed such vision as to see the purpose of the visit, the warning coming toward her like a speeding, brakeless train.

"Hello," said the schoolteacher, walking straight toward her with her hand extended, flat open, like a wooden plank.

"Kako ste?" asked the mother. She knew a greeting was required but all the while she was thinking, *What do you want from me?*

"Your daughter's missed school for five consecutive days." The teacher held up her hand, splayed the five fingers, then touched each one. The truant daughter came out from behind a bush. In the classroom she always hid in the background, was smart enough to position herself behind the wall of eager children with their hands raised, faces turned toward the teacher like flowers to sunlight.

The teacher raised her voice a little. "Your daughter is truant—do you understand the word, 'truant?' " She spelled the word out loud, as if the spelling, the emphasis on each letter would speed the translation, as if only that word needed to be translated over the others, was any more difficult than "do" or "you" or "understand" or "word."

The daughter translated for her mother: "Your daughter is a star."

The mother looked the teacher up and down, the navy blue suit, the pressed white collar. There was something about the way the teacher stood, nose held high, as if the world owed her a living.

"She will be expelled if she does not return," the teacher said, and then pointed to the daughter and gave a motion like she was throwing something out—a basin of water, a bag of trash.

The mother knew what the gesture meant: The teacher was judging her. Another thought passed through her: *This woman wants my daughter, my son.* The only real things she possessed.

Silence can be more instructive than any lesson plan. If you listen closely you can hear the conversations of trees, the daily discourse of evergreen and elm, the rumors they spread, or can hear the deep confessions in the sound of the train, stories of heartbreak retold on every mile of track. If you listen closely you can hear people's thoughts sometimes, what they keep hidden: a desire to be loved at all costs, the running tab of hurts and betrayals, each person's grocery list of needs.

The mother twisted the shovel deeper into the dirt. For hours every day they took her children away—to learn what? What did they teach them that was useful? Was her daughter shown how to dry a cod for bakalar or crochet a warm blanket for a sick child? Was her son taught a trade, to fish like his ancestors before him, taught the hard lessons of the sea? With work to be done and her husband long gone and the mortgage to pay and the wash and garden—with all this and no man, what good was school? What could they learn there that would help them get by? These thoughts rolled and built up in her, rubbed together and created friction, and the heat of the thoughts left her body and scorched the teacher's neat white collar and wilted the nearby vines.

Perhaps it was that very heat that now surrounded the schoolteacher or the hot sun that beat down in the late afternoon. What is it that combines to cause a person to feel that they are suffering some indignity? What combination of thoughts or weather or feelings or season finally forces a hand? The teacher took out a record book and shoved it toward the mother's face, showed her the attendance marks, little Xs for each day a student missed. The march of marks after the daughter's name carried across the entire page of the ledger and looked like the black Xs the mother made on the welfare forms, the one script she had mastered.

Cold begets cold. Heat begets heat. "Dovoljno, dovoljno!" the mother cried: *Enough, enough!* She jumped up and made shooing motions with her hands that translate in any language: go back to where you came from, go away. "Mislis da ja cu bit chee chee," she screamed. "Mislis da ja cu bit chee chee!"

The daughter threw back her head and laughed, and the schoolteacher, freshly offended, commanded her to translate.

"Chee-chee!" the daughter cried. And because the teacher did not understand, she shouted, "Teacher! Chee chee! My mother says, why do I need to go to school? You think I'm going to be a teacher?"

The mother, as if understanding every word of the translation, let out a whoop and laughed and she and her daughter jumped up and down and began to sing in unison, "Mislis da ja cu bit chee chee!" waving their arms in the air as if shooing away crows.

The teacher left and never returned. The truant son bought a boat and there were fish, plenty of fish, plenty of food to eat. The truant daughter stayed home, tended the garden, and learned to grow food instead of words. The plums grew plentiful, as did spinach and squash and tomatoes, a profusion of vegetables. Dandelions carpeted the grass and turned it golden. The earth bloomed, as if the teacher provided acid to alkaline soil. Like fish bones turned into fertilizer, her visit was ground up and reused.

Letter from Croatia: Bog i Hrvati

IN SPLIT, EVERYTHING IS NOTED. AT THE OUTDOOR MARKET, near a souvenir stand, a woman is talking with a security guard when I approach, as marked a tourist as you'll ever see in my travelware: stiff new walking shoes, Serbo-Croatian phrase book, a money belt adding a tire around my waist like a little beer belly. The woman gives the guard a nod, a check-this-out, and he straightens up a bit, gets official. He's a thin man in a white shirt with navy blue epaulets, a step down from the government soldiers who patrol the wet streets in their damp khaki. Even though he is wearing the wrong color, the security guard still has that air of petit power. I've seen it all over the country, this need by the powerless to lord something over someone.

I encountered something similar earlier in the day, while waiting in a long line at the Jadrolinja ferry office. I wanted information on how to get out of Croatia. My ticket for departure was at midnight, it was twelve hours until then but I wanted to leave now. I was starting to feel the country might blow again, that it was on the verge of reconfiguring. A ticket agent told me the ferries had temporarily stopped running, and so I decided to stay put and wait it out. If everything was in flux it seemed best to be ready for any opening. I turned from the ticket counter, from the sign with the ferry's motto in English—THANK YOU FOR TRUSTING US—and noticed there were no chairs or benches in the reception room. No place to wait in a country where—since the war—all people do is wait. I found a window ledge wide enough to sit on and slumped down. The next thing I felt was a sharp jolt, then another, awoke to find a short, stocky man kicking my shoe. No sleeping here, he mimed, then hitched up his trousers and cockwalked away, chest puffed up and out. Here, everyone does a little impersonation of Tito.

The market woman whispers something to the guard and I know I need to make a connection. I offer up "Dobro jutro," good morning, one of the few salutations I know. She counters with a curt "Dobar dan," good afternoon, and then there is a lull. I wonder if she can see kinship. Though it's obvious from these trappings that I am an American tourist, I'm also a third generation Croat. Both sets of grandparents came from the Dalmatian coast, from islands I've just visited. If she looks straight at me she will see the identifiable trademarks: that thick, thick head of hair you find on so many Slavs, the large facial features. There's no aquiline nose, no porcelain skin, no fineness of feature. If she recognizes anything, she's not letting on, just looks away and pretends to straighten the postcards.

I start to do what I've been doing the entire trip, cross-referencing with my culture as a way to make the strange familiar. If she smiled she'd look like an Eastern European Rosemary Clooney, the same jowly cheeks, the jazz-club eyes. I picture her singing "Come On-A My House," but it doesn't quite work. Given the war, who knows where her house is—or *if* it is. And that type of magnanimous gesture, an invitation to come on over, only happened in Italy, where buon giornos rained down from every stoop. Here, I'm greeted with suspicion at every turn.

The wind starts up. Colored plastic flags that circle the market make sounds in the air like small slaps. Though it's mid-July, there's talk of a storm on its way, moving east across Europe. Today's paper reports that yesterday in Tuscany flash floods swept through the summer fields, taking people under without warning. The forecast only adds to the sense of peril, the sense of something closing in. Maybe the storm will wash out the false boundaries, the lines that separate Croatia from Bosnia from Serbia—once Yugoslavia and before that Austria and before that something else. If one thing's clear it's that every inch of the ground below us is capable of shift.

I take in what the woman has to offer. There are souvenir trinkets and lots of things that look "beachy": neon-orange sand buckets, green flip-flops, ceramic salt and pepper shakers embossed with pictures of Split. Everything spells seaside and gaiety and abandon, elements that come with any riviera. I rifle through a box and find a postcard of the church I passed on the way to the market but without its present scaffolding, the exposed corset of pipes and catwalks that surround the structure. When I first saw the church I thought it was in the middle of a historic restoration, the remedy for centuries of wear and tear. On closer look, I noticed the church tower was blackened, pockmarked by shells—a souvenir from when the Serbs bombed the port.

I finger a deck of cards painted with scenes of the Dalmatian coast, then put it back. I want to make a quick decision but can't seem to move—it's as if my bones have locked up. In the past three days I've started to feel trapped. The two-week trip to find some ancestral connection has gone on a little too long, in truth, has gone sour, and no matter how much cross-referencing I do, this isn't my world. I expected to be welcomed with open arms, certain the people here would recognize kin. After hearing about the old country all my life and watching *Croatian Magazine* on the cable channel, I thought it would be so easy: another version of the prodigal daughter comes home. I expected a merry people, as if the war had never happened, as if years of communist rule and collusion with despots hadn't had any effect and were only the creations of some over-active conservative imagination.

All I know is, I hadn't expected this. Wherever I go, people first give me a tense, furtive look and then glance away, their faces turning inward. It reminds me of my friends back home and their first response to the trip, a response I couldn't fathom.

⚓   ⚓   ⚓

When I told people I was going to Croatia, conversation stopped. Friends looked into their glasses of Campari or shots of grappa, the Italian digestivi I was serving to help them digest it all. I waited for the bump in interest that usually marks any comment about a trip, a string of questions that would allow me to puff and swell, the proud explorer. But there was nothing. Some didn't even bother to ask why, they simply went silent and then switched to another topic.

I knew what they are thinking: What strange psychology prompted my urge to visit a place full of mass graves? Who would travel halfway around the world to rubberneck a war? They eyed me differently from then on, and the talk suffered. It's like when you tell someone you're sick, how my colleague Deborah told me at the lunch wagon, "Oh, did you survive your classes, advising day was pure hell, and, by the way, I have lymphoma." The conversation took a turn. I wondered about her then, a person who could slip it in so casually, thrown in like an aside, like what to get for dinner. Who wouldn't wait a moment for emphasis, or to simply let others catch their breath, while screwing up the courage to ask the unthinkable? Which—when you're referring to the former Yugoslavia—is the every day.

But I wanted my friends to understand. Though none of my generation had ever set foot on that soil it was where we were from. If we were to trace roots there would be one long arc, a thick crayon line across this country, the Atlantic, Western Europe, over the Adriatic, and then straight to the Dalmatian coast. It was only another short crayon length to where the fighting was now.

For me, the war served as impetus. If I didn't get there quick, who knew who or what would be left?

⚓ ⚓ ⚓

It's starting to drizzle hard. I still need something to bring back home, something to show my people that our people are carrying on. All my relatives will be looking for the bottle of Slivovitz or a handmade lace tablecloth. I finger a bumper sticker that has a Croatian coat of arms in national colors. The background of the shield sports a red and white checkerboard, in a Purina Dog Chow pattern, and surrounding the shield there's a saber, a ram, and another animal that looks like an ocelot. Above the shield is a message in bold script: BOG I HVRATI. Does it mean something akin to "I Love New York," without the heart, or maybe "Love I Croatians," the syntax shifted, the grammar skewed? Out of nowhere I remember my grandmother's voice in prayer, remember that "Bog" is "God." The Croatian "i" must be "and." At first it seems too easy, *God and Croatians,* and I'm disappointed that the country would fall to jingoism so quickly. But why should it be any different here? Everyone appropriates. There's God and Germany, God and the Sunshine State, God and the Tarheels. Maybe it's Croatia's turn. Even my mother, while watching *Jeopardy,* wants parity. If one contestant is losing, is too slow on the buzzer, she shouts at the others on the panel, "Oh, for Christ's sake, let the little guy win."

The woman clears her throat, and suddenly I get it: reverie is luxury. I quickly settle on the bumper sticker. She holds out her palm and I give her ten kuna. The paper money seems fragile, easy to tear. I can't count the change she gives back, just notice that there is some. There is another lull and then I say, cheerily, "Sretan put," another salutation I've heard somewhere, something people here have said to me. "Carry on" is what I believe it to mean, or "Here's to you." The woman snickers and the security guard laughs and then says, mockingly, "Oh, Sretan put! Sretan put!" but spits out "put"each time. They give each other a knowing look.

I don't want to know what they know. I turn away and look toward the port, can see the large car ferry waiting there in the distance fueling, up. Its eight more hours till departure, until I'm on my way back across the Adriatic to safe, forgiving Italy. The guard coughs to draw my attention, then pulls up his pants, the bully's universal sign.

⚓   ⚓   ⚓

When I was in the town of Vela Luka, on the island of Korcula, the place of my grandmother's birth, I found a woman with my last name. The search for origins wasn't as hard as I'd imagined. My family name was everywhere. There was an empty electronics shop with the sign MIROSE-VIC'S RADIONICA above the locked door. A Mirosevic ran the camera store.

In the graveyard I found a nest of potential cousins, aunts, and great-great relations. There were other familiar surnames as well. There was a Buric who must be related to my mother's friend Winny Burich, who had the skinny daughter, Mary Margaret. There was a Pesic, a sure relative of the Slav my family called "the Foreigner," the Pesich who fished with my father and had that thick accent that refused to lessen over time. As I walked through the graveyard I read the first names out loud: Ante and Ivo and Freda and Mirka. Here were all the ones I didn't get to soon enough.

The islands were different from what I had pictured. I'd been told the landscape was beautiful beyond measure—the sea a bluer blue, the Mediterranean light washing everything golden. For a while, the picture held true. When the ferry pulled in to port, from the deck I could see palm trees lining the streets, quaint old hotels along the quay shuttered against the sunlight, hand-painted sailboats in the harbor. Above the town, low green hills were covered in olive trees, and the white rocky soil looked lit from within.

The trick was to not look too closely. I walked off the ferry, the only tourist to grace the dock, and there were none of the welcoming faces to greet me that I found in Italy, grandmotherly types offering cheap shelter for the night. The men on board pushed me aside to rush down the gang-plank without reason or apology. (It wouldn't dawn on me until later that when there is so little, you push for what you need.) As I walked into the town I noticed the hotels weren't shuttered up for the afternoon siesta but were boarded up, and the windows that weren't boarded were broken out. Stores looked permanently closed, the foodstuffs in the windows graying on display. Everywhere there was lack. Women whispered to each other as I passed, and the men who sat idle outside the bars hushed.

After asking around I found a living Mirosevic, a Croatian woman named Melita. When I told her my name she wrapped me up in her arms and wouldn't let go. There must have been some genealogical link between us, deep rooted, and even though we couldn't locate it in the church record of births and deaths, we both felt as if we'd found kin. There was that shirt-off-your-back type of trust, immediate and genuine, and once the connection was made she proceeded to take me around the town and show me off. People who scowled at me when I first came off the ferry now smiled and clucked in a proprietary way. It felt like the stuff of movies, like some Capra movie reunion scene, family connection with the mere saying of a name, no need to prove anything else to win affection.

After I met every possible fifth cousin, Melita wanted to show me her summer home. She insisted. We drove over the dry hills, passed men in hay carts and women in black shawls, picturesque and desperate, until we came to a small cove dotted with white stucco homes. She parked the car and led me down a stone path to what she called "my little villa." Her house was small by American standards—a one-bedroom cottage with a shore view—but it wasn't the size that was important. A summerhouse was a sign of prosperity. She wanted to show off, to show me, her long-lost American relative, that she was doing well, that people did well, it wasn't all bleak.

As we walked back up the path, back toward the car, I noticed the large brick home next to hers for the first time. All the windows were blown out, as if someone had taken target practice. It looked like the crackhouse on my street back home. There was graffiti I couldn't read marking the brick, the scrawl all angles and exclamation points. Emphasis is the same in any language. I asked her whose house it was.

"Oh, a Serb doctor lived there. They aren't coming back." She gave a quick uncomfortable laugh and then went silent. At first I thought I had reminded her of a common quarrel with a neighbor, some falling out over a property line or how one party felt miffed at not getting an invitation to the other's daughter's wedding. Still, a neighborly row that could be fixed with some wine and apology. But it was deeper than that, more raw. It's as if I had reminded her of the worst kind of betrayal, the kind where you can't even hear the person's name again without chilling. It's a person you used to have over day or night, who had your house key, who learned about your crazy sister and the strange family histories and had seen you at your worst, not generous and loving, but petty and wrong. They hold those secrets about you and you don't have any control of them anymore. Now they're out in the world without loyalty or bond to hold them in check.

I asked her, "Do you think it will ever be repaired?" But she was either too far ahead of me on the path or she pretended not to hear. Or maybe she was trying to figure out which I meant: the relationship or the house or the country.

⚓   ⚓   ⚓

Over at the ferry building cafe, I eat one last pizza. I spread my mementos out in front of me: the bumper sticker, a small block of granite I found by a Mirosevic grave, a bottle of amber liqueur, the color of the dandelion wine my grandmother used to make. There's the rose the new relative gave me, already dried up and flaking dark red. I count out the remaining currency that no other country will cash, the European neighbors' vote of no confidence in the new regime. Outside the cafe window, on the patio that overlooks the ferries, the trees are going sideways, the sea churning out fast gray waves with whitecaps that look like hankies on top.

I'd been to this cafe when I first came to Split, at the start of the adventure, and journey proud. Even then I noticed that the place was a little grim. It had flimsy tables and a large, empty banquet room with all the place settings set out, but I had the sense no one was coming. I ordered a beer and a pizza from a dark-haired waitress named Zorka. When I asked her "Kako ste?" she raised her arms wide and answered, "Beautiful! My life is beautiful." I wanted to believe her but it all seemed a bit forced, like how, at the start of her TV show, Mary Tyler Moore threw her hat up in the air and you were supposed to think it was a moment of abandon in Mary's stiff little life.

On that day there was only one other family in the place, the parents ordering orangeades for the kids, cautioning them to sip slowly while the kids eyed my pizza. Zorka brought out a picture book and explained to me that she had a second job. Inside the book were photographs of decorative cakes. There were wedding cakes, baptismal cakes. One cake was in the shape of a race car, another in the shape of church bells. She announced that she was about to show me her prizewinner and then she turned the page and with a kind of reverence, whispered "Minnie Mouse." I noticed that Minnie had on that cakey polka-dot skirt and the funny shoes, but she still looked Slav to me, her hairdo thick and out of control.

Today, my waiter is a young man named Dragan. With his sparse goatee, he looks like a skinny beatnik. We strike up a conversation and I find out that he once had a six-month travel visa and lived in Greenwich Village. I tell him about my last two weeks, the trips to the islands. When I ask him why people have given me the cold shoulder, have been initially so suspicious, he says gently, "They thought you were a Serb. Or a friend of a Serb come to check on property left behind. Everyone is suspect until identified. You have to look *behind* the gestures."

I tell him about the relatives, about the graveyard. What I don't tell him is that I've had enough of the old country. If there's one thing I've come to understand it's the urge to depart. But maybe he can feel it too. He says he wants desperately to go home to Vukovar but can't, just as I want to go home to San Francisco right now but can't—at least not for a few hours. When he says the word Vukovar it's with such tenderness, such softness that it sounds as if he is be talking about a loved one, some person he wants to protect.

Maybe his softness makes me feel that I can ask him what I haven't been able to ask anyone else on the trip, a direct question about the war. "Do you think it's over now?"

I can see him flinch a little, revisit a pain. Why do I feel it would be good for him to talk about it—another cross-reference—a kind of political psychotherapy? As if we're on some global talk show and, as host, I lean the mike towards him and say, "Go ahead, get the war off your chest."

He says, "Some people don't want to forgive or forget." I'm left for a moment trying to figure out the difference. Does forgiveness allow you to forget, or is it the other way around: the ability to forget allows you to forgive what's been done to you? Isn't there usually some kind of choice involved, pick one or the other, or do you get to say no to both options?

I think about the summer house again.

I ask him if he'd like to return to the U.S., just until things stabilize here.

"I can't get another visa," he says, then adds, "None of us can leave." He picks up my empty glass, turns toward the kitchen, then turns back.

He speaks slowly. "Why would I want to leave everything I have?" He gives me a fierce look, one I won't debate. A look that says there's something I'm not getting. "This is where I am from," he says and spreads his arms wide to the horizon, to the harbor and the hills beyond, to the open market and the men marching the streets.

I look, too, at the port of departure where you can't depart, as landlocked as if you're far inland, miles from the sea and maybe that's when it hits me. What if you can't leave but don't want to leave? What if you can't go forward and you can't go back? It's stasis that's the most damaging. It's the inability to move. You're stuck here, with that neighbor over there across the new line, glaring at you, the one who loved you, the one you once loved. What are you going to do with each other, how will you find a way back or find relations again or find solution or find escape? It's not that I haven't felt that mix of emotions, a pull to embrace and a pull to flee. But there's a difference between Dragan and me. I have a ticket out.

I try to imagine when Split was beautiful and easy, when there wasn't a startle response. I look out the window at the sea, now whipping up. The glass keeps us safe, keeps the sound out. It gets quiet enough between us for me to notice an American rock band is on the cafe loudspeakers. I ask him who it is.

"Nirvana." His look says he's surprised I don't know. I haven't the heart to tell him that, in a weird way, Kurt Cobain wanted to leave too.

When I finish my meal and get ready to pay, he touches me on the arm, says, "Please wait." He walks back to the kitchen. Maybe he has a picture book too, a sideline business. I can't imagine Dragan as an entrepreneur, but in the new Croatia, who has a choice?

When he returns he's carrying a small white plate. The boss of the cafe, a big man in a dirty apron, watches from the back room. Everything is noted. Dragan sets down the plate on the blue tablecloth. I notice there are two mints offered up, free, unordered. He beams at me, aware of the chance he's taking, this generosity in the face of reprimand, then leans over and whispers, "Sretan put."

I ask him to translate and he says, "It means good luck on your travels. It means have a good trip."

Long Live Our Side

THE AP PHOTO SHOWS AN OLD WOMAN DANCING ON THE SEVERED wing of a downed Stealth bomber. The woman looks to be about seventy, has a kerchief tied around her hair. She is wearing knit stockings and heavy wool socks, like my grandmother wore; she has a woolen sweater-vest over her dress and an apron over that, like my grandmother wore. She is waving a bottle of brandy in the air, having a big time. When someone asks her how she feels about the Serbs downing an American fighter, she answers, "Long live our side."

⚓   ⚓   ⚓

Before the name Milosevic was unloosed on the world, pronounced and mispronounced many times a day, my last name elicited the typically confused responses one expects with any other ethnic-sounding name. "What kind of name is that? Czech? Polish?" But nothing too dramatic. Each benign encounter—making a doctor's appointment, calling for a reservation—began with a spelling lesson: "Okay, ready now," I'd say as if I were preparing them for a long ordeal. "M-i-r-o-s—as in Sam—e-v—as in vegetables (since converting to pacifism, I'd switched from V as in victor)—i-c-h." Usually there would be a little laugh on the other end of the line, then some acknowledgment, a low whistle. "That's a long one," they'd say, and I could tell a bond had formed, as if we'd gotten through something together.

Now when I spell out the name there's silence. I want to preface the spelling with "It's the same name I've always had." Only now the name connotes ethnic cleansing. These days, I'm extra careful. One slip of the tongue and the names are identical.

I tell my friends that it's like having the name Edith Amin, or A. Hitner. Mirosevich. Milosevic. It's awful damn close.

It took me awhile to understand the repercussions. I pick up my tax return from the people at Tax Time and the secretary with the Dutch accent who has seen my name for years—on W-2 forms, on the check I sign over for services rendered—peers above her half-glasses, a scrutinizing gaze, and asks, "Oh, Toni. Your name . . . is it . . . Russian?"

As innocent as snowfall.

"Mirosevich?" As if I've heard the name myself for the first time, a little uncomfortable sounding in the mouth, something to mispronounce. "Mirrrrosevich?" I say it again, this time emphasizing the difference, rolling the R, giving it a Spanish pronunciation. "No, it's Croatian." And then a pause, a quick step. "My relatives came from Croatia, both sides," so there's no question of origin. And then I begin to go into history, detailed information about the family tree, town names, Croatian phrases—more intimate about my past than I usually am with tax-preparation people.

Still, there's a wariness. The tax preparer, a smallish woman with a head for numbers, comes out of her cubicle; then the young filing person, a high-school student, enters from the back room. A tribunal forms, the three of them forming a half-circle on the beige carpet, blocking the exit door. I tell them I visited Croatia three years ago. I threaten to bring back pictures of the trip. I say I found the name Mirosevich all over the cemetery in a Croatian village. They laugh uneasily. How much evidence will they need?

The air has gotten prickly. Just give me the goddamned tax return, I want to say. But any heightened voice, any sudden move, will be seen as aggression. Something tells me I better watch my step. None of this is making sense. I don't remember this fierce need to legitimize, the need to chart lineage, to claim an alliance with the right side, our side?

That night I call my sister, two states away, for some verification.

"When we were young, were there such distinctions? I don't ever recall anyone being called a Serb or a Croat or a Bosnian. Could it be our parents knew who was who, but it simply didn't filter down? Weren't we all just Slavs?" Even now I can picture our seacoast town, Everett, full of dark green trees and salt air, not unlike the Dalmatian coast, the islands of the Pacific Northwest mirror images of the islands of Hvar, Brac. In America the Slav fishermen shared the world with Norwegians, the other ethnicity on the docks—with their Viking stance and boats with names like Northern Lights and Arctic Song. They seemed so self-contained, so inward, compared to us.

"Oh, no, everyone was Croatian," she alleges. "All the fishermen, all the relatives. People just didn't feel the need to say."

Is our memory selective? Was everyone 100 percent the same?

I wish I had learned the language. When I was young, the men would gather around the table after dinner and yell in Serbo-Croatian. I knew enough to make out that one of the old men was a partisan, which sounded dangerous and fun. I heard the name Tito so often I thought he was an uncle.

Only years later, as an adult, having dinner with some Russian immigrants, did I learn different. That night I offered what I thought was a simple solution for the crisis: "We need a Tito to bring the country back together again." I was surprised to hear Vladimir hiss, "Tito, the butcher." He then gave me a revised history lesson, tales long into the night, of repression, of Tito's iron rule.

If I didn't quite know the language or the history, something else did get through. What I do remember is some kind of ethnic pride at any Slav, any "ich" doing well in the world. Reading the sports page my father would spot a Matulich or a Sevenich, a car dealer or maybe some coach who took his basketball team to the city finals, and he'd yell, "Hey, look, another Slav." We'd stop what we were doing, gather around him to read the name in print. As if we knew him personally. Almost a relative. Almost a neighbor. Our kind was doing well in the world. Even today, Shots has taken this on. When movie credits roll, she'll see a name, Bozich. "Hey, look," she'll say, "the best boy's a Slav," happy to have spotted it first.

It was how the world was defined. If not as divisive as us and them, then at least as noted as us and others. But it was a big "us," an inclusive us, and anyone with the right suffix was in.

Now I know better. "We're Croatian," I tell the secretary. "Or more specifically, Dalmatian. All the family emigrated from the islands; Dugi Otok and Korcula."

A few years ago, I began receiving cards from my American relatives announcing a slew of family reunions. Someone was feeling nostalgic. The cards often pictured a man and woman on the front in traditional Dalmatian dress—white flowing skirts and blouses, embroidered vests with a vaguely Turkish look. Inside there was some tired joke about dogs. "First we were Slavs, then Croatians, now we're 101 Dalmatians!"

I never did tell them that when I visited Dalmatia I was surprised by the lack of welcome. I didn't want to mention that when I arrived in my grandparents' town of Vela Luka and asked about the family name at an outdoor cafe, I was pointed to the cemetery ("groblje"). As I stumbled through my Serbo-Croatian phrase book in an attempt to get the directions, the waitress asked in perfect English why I didn't know my people's language. She was skeptical, as if I was covering something up, was really a Serb in disguise. I told her I only knew bits of songs and swear words learned on the docks. I didn't tell her the one phrase that stuck, jebem ti boga, to fuck god. She listened to my excuses, then shook her head and said, "It is your parents' sin."

I left the cafe and walked up a dirt lane toward the low stonewalls of the groblje. Once inside the gates it felt like old home week. There they were, all the names, all the familiar clan, the original recipe, and on one grave Toni Mirosevic—only the "h" missing. A little chill, a link. How could we not be related? Later, I looked in the church registry, and, with the help of the English-speaking priest, found that some of the original Miroseviches, a name as common as Smith, came from Montenegro. Montenegrin? I thought we were a sea people, saline in the blood. Who is pure? If we want to be clear on who's who, we'd better do some research.

The caption said LONG LIVE OUR SIDE. Well, which is our side? And will that change tomorrow? And how fiercely do I need to claim to be me and not you and a friend told me if that son of a bitch of a neighbor doesn't keep his hedge from growing onto her property she's going to kill him, and I notice, in the tax office, how the secretary has a Dutch flag on her computer and how the particle walls are set at angles so no one ever really has to see the person who sits three feet away.

The tribunal stands firm, stone-faced, impassive. What sentence will they impose? Will they tip the auditor when I leave, plaster my returns on the Internet?

This is what I want to tell them: I cry when I see the Kosovars in those long lines. I cry when I see Serbians in the rubble of an errant cruise missile. I cry when I see Bosnian refugees here in San Francisco. I cry when I think of the Croatian relatives on the islands with the same last name. I cry for all of them, for that one and that one and that one. Messy tears, indiscriminate tears. All over the map.

How do you spell it? M as in missiles—i-r—as in reconnaissance—o-s—as in stealth—e-v-i-c—as in carnage—h—as in hell.

Somehow I don't think this is going to wash with the tribunal. Just as I know this won't wash with the politicians, the political analysts, the pundits. I know this won't wash with so many—the way pacifism didn't wash with the Marxists in my anti-nuclear group so many years ago. "I don't believe in killing," I would tell them, my blanket philosophy. "But what's your theory about the masses?" they'd ask, incredulous that my analysis was so weak.

I think back to how easily they accepted me into the group because of the name Mirosevich—how commie sounding, how un-American. A name that provided a certain entry into radical communities, certainly more than Carnegie or Rockefeller would have.

The woman in the picture looks like my grandmother. I remember Nana well, happy to be here, happy to not be back in the old country, yet torn to not be home. When I have told people about growing up in a Slav community I often say: Everyone was like us. I didn't realize until now that not knowing the divisions was a blessing. As Stein might have put it: a Slav was a Slav was a Slav.

It was the only world I knew. Once, from a print interview, I wrote down something the writer Jamaica Kincaid said. It went something like this: "You grow up on a street and it's a tiny street. The street may not be as big as this yard out there. But it becomes your world. It's the only thing you know and you know it unbelievably well with this thickness, this heaviness, and you have no interest in anything else. It would not occur to you that there might be something else."

It's what she knows. It's what we know. Our side, our turf, my block, my name.

Years ago I heard a story. I don't even recall the beginning, the middle, or the end. There were two Slav antagonists, there was a conflict, something was at stake. One person says to the other, "If I live long, you live short."

The secretary breaks rank, tired, or bored, or ready to go home, and hands over the forms. On the cover it reads: Mirosevich, Tax Year, 1998. Below the preparer's name: Thank you for the privilege of serving you.

Long live our side, I want to tell her, long live your side. Maybe better, long live us and them.

The Bullet

THAT I WAS TOO CLEAN-SCRUBBED, TOO VANILLA, FOR THE rough Southern California high school I'd transferred to was obvious. My shining apple look—from growing up in the Northwest—didn't fit in San Pedro, California, once described as a grimy harbor town where tough girls teased or ratted their hair into high palaces that challenged the laws of physics. I'd heard that one girl hid razor blades in her hair so rivals would cut their hands during hair-pulling catfights and that the ice cream man, in his white van, was hauled away for selling reds (downers) along with the Nutty Buttys. Having never taken so much as a puff from a cigarette it was obvious what an odd duck I was.

What was less obvious was that I was an odd duck with a hidden talent, one that was about to force me into the spotlight, center stage, the elevated playing field of high school fame.

There *was* a slightly elevated playing field at San Pedro High, where the drill team practiced their energetic formations every afternoon. Their job was cheering the football team—the San Pedro Pirates—on to victory, in gold and black uniform jumpers, one seductive hoop earring dangling from each right ear lobe. During halftime the drill team would take the field and form semi-recognizable shapes: a pirate ship or skull and bones. Once they formed a pirate's face complete with eye patch, though one section of the formation lost a step, which resulted in a pirate with a facial droop, Captain Hook afflicted with some form of palsy.

I joined the team because this upbeat regimented outdoor activity was reminiscent of other upbeat regimented outdoor activities in the Northwest: marching up Mount Rainier, running speed trials in the rain. Still, I was deeply depressed in this new milieu and tried not to show it. It was probably that effort to put on a happy face that changed my fate. One afternoon, while waiting for practice to begin, I leapt up, ran a short distance and turned a hand flip, something I'd known how to do since I was a child, my body jackknifing end over end, until I landed on my feet with a stick, both arms raised high, like an Olympic gymnast. Someone saw me and took note. Word got back to the drill team captain, a mannish girl whom I secretly desired and feared.

That afternoon the team was to practice forming a gun. We'd already done a pirate's scabbard, a cannonball. Maybe we were moving on to more modern weaponry. Maybe there was a secret agenda by the hawkish school administration to support the war raging in Vietnam. Maybe the rationale was that we'd start with a pistol and move up to M-16s, rocket launchers, then go nuclear with ICBMs. Either way, our next challenge was to form a gun with a recognizable handle, trigger, chamber and barrel. And in the center, running down the barrel to burst onto the field and hit the mark, the target, was to be one bullet.

A bullet who could turn hand flips.

The next week at school my status rose as swiftly as a black flag flying up a mast. I was now simply known as The Bullet. As in, "Hey, here comes The Bullet." As in "What's up, Big B?" My teachers, recognizing the pressure that comes with overnight fame, let me out of class early so I could get to the field and practice, turning flips over and over again, with military precision.

⚓   ⚓   ⚓

On the night of the big game the sky was clear, the weather balmy. A trade wind off the ocean sent the palm trees stirring while the stars shone above. I was about to take my place in that firmament. The bleachers were full of Slav relatives: my mother, aunts, uncles, second cousins. My own claque. I knew they were thinking *One of our own has risen*. No doubt this would warrant a mention in *The Croatia Times* or even make its way back to the old country.

At halftime, our team was losing. The Pirates often lost, ending games without having pillaged and burned a single point. We were the girls behind the boys and knew our mission. We took the field.

The gun began to take shape. Girls formed the handle, the barrel. Three girls held hands and formed the little trigger. I walked to the center, into the chamber, and waited for a drumroll, my signal to run down the barrel toward the large butcher-paper target two girls held up at barrel's end. I was to flip through the paper while two others turned on fire extinguishers to simulate gunsmoke. At that exact moment a band member would pound on a bass drum, one booming shot heard 'round the world.

The drumroll started. The drill captain gave me an adoring smile, a thumbs-up. I took off. I couldn't hear a thing except for the wind in the palms, my breath. I ran down the barrel of the gun as fast as I could, though I felt I was running in a dream, in slow motion, struggling against a powerful headwind. I saw the target ahead, the white square of paper upon which I would write the story of my rise to power, a small white square that grew larger the nearer I got, now, the white covering my entire field of vision. *Now. Jump now.* I put my hands out, ready to dive and flip as I'd never flipped.

I ran through the paper. There was a scream. Maybe it was my mother.

There was no flip. I lost my courage. Either that or I blacked out as I ran through the white plane.

I stopped. I stood there. I looked behind me and saw the tatters of butcher paper. The fire extinguishers, waiting for the flip, never sprayed. The drummer, waiting for his cue, never made a sound.

The next week in school my fame disappeared. "The Bullet's a dud," I heard someone say. One of the cattier girls on the drill team said, "Any yahoo could have *run* through the goddamned paper."

One day while I was eating lunch alone under a palm tree, one of the school freaks came over and gave me a copy of Joan Baez's autobiography, *Daybreak.* I knew what the gesture meant. The freaks had accepted me. My new role as pariah gave me elevated status with the outcasts. In the book Baez wrote, "My life is a crystal teardrop." I knew exactly how that felt. From that day on I vowed, like Baez, to become a pacifist. I grew my hair long and wore clunky tire-tread sandals. Flip-less. I joined the anti-war marches though I didn't tell anyone I had any special skills. I was against the Vietnam War, then Desert Storm, now the war in Iraq. I've never owned a gun.

The Nutria

There is no separation in that land beyond the sky.
—from "We Shall All Be Reunited"

IT WAS BECOMING MORE DIFFICULT TO STAY IN THE MOMENT.

I was out on a morning walk on the San Andreas Trail to test out my new philosophy du jour. The name of the trail and its reference to a major San Francisco Bay Area fault line might give some people pause. People on edge. The trail exists as a warning. An omen. A reminder of our temporal existence. Here the world can break open at a moment's notice. I had been reading a book on Buddhism and thought it was a philosophy that could serve me at this midpoint in my life. I was looking for a hand or a leg up on my current list of worries: the mortgage, the latest study on osteoporosis, what to do with the recent gossip about a coworker's hot indiscretion. You can become so encumbered, so weighted down with worry about what happened yesterday at the office, or last week, or some inequity that occurred when you were twelve, that you can barely put one foot in front of the other, you can barely move. This can prevent ever being fully present, in the moment. That, in a nutshell, was what the book was about. One of the tenets of the philosophy, as I read it, was that if a person could only *stay* in the moment there was a nice payoff: you would be able to see that there was no separation between this moment and the next, this world and the next. If you could truly live in the moment you could have access to all of it, past, present and future, time immemorial. Wouldn't that ease the daily load?

Maybe part of the difficulty was that I hadn't gotten very far in the book. I gave it a quick surface read, skimmed the chapters on "Renunciation," "The Four Noble Truths," and moved quickly toward the back of the book, toward "Enlightenment." Given that I was speed-reading, retention was minimal. Some might say I was only applying the philosophy skin-deep, that mine was merely a topical application of Buddhism. But isn't some covering better than none? Couldn't even a thin application serve as a kind of spiritual hand cream or sunscreen against ennui? Protection was necessary, given that the sun was piercing through the clouds and the ozone, shining down through that big invisible hole in the sky, beating down on the path, on me, and on the blue waters of the reservoir glittering at my right. There was a warm, brisk wind that raced across the water so that the blue of the lake served as the background canvas for a whole band of moving white checkpoints of light, reminding me of the glassy ponds that adorn special birthday cakes, say the kind of cake made for an outdoors-type Dad, with a fishing lake and tiny little marzipan evergreen trees and HAPPY BIRTHDAY TO THE WORLD'S BEST FISHER-MAN written on top with icing. The reservoir waters had that same sheen, like cooked sugar.

But there I was again, not in the moment, back in childhood, in Everett, Washington, my birthplace, standing inside the B and M Bakery, my face pushed up against the glass display bakery cases, staring at the novelty cakes hanging suspended on glass shelves. I caught myself up short and tried to recall the instructions for meditation detailed in the book. When this leaping out of the moment occurred, one was told to label that "thinking." I said the word out loud, "thinking," but maybe just a bit too harshly, as one might say "Hey buddy, get the hell back in your lane" to a wayward driver, a little sharp scolding, which is what the Buddhist nun, who wrote the book, explicitly told me not to do.

Still, a good reprimand can have its merits. Momentarily I returned to where I was. There they were again, the reservoir's blue waters, but then I thought not of this moment but of another time when I thought I was in the moment, not distracted by cake metaphors or memory.

⚓ ⚓ ⚓

Shots and I were in Italy, at the tail end of a summer trip that took us across the country, first to the Ligurian coast on the Italian Riviera, then to Siena during the heat of Ferragosto, down south through Tuscany and back again to Florence where we first began. The whole of the month of August was hot, hotter than Hades, the Hades Luca Signorelli painted on the walls of the Duomo in Orvieto, all fire and furnace, the kind of heat that would be oppressive if you weren't in Florence and dammit, I don't care how hot the thermometer says it is, this is Florence, seat of the Renaissance, the origin of Western art and let's have a good time. We spent the final days of vacation walking the city, buying perfume at Santa Maria Novella, eating as much spinaci saltati as possible, the saltiest spinach ever prepared, and trying to analyze why the Italians seemed so in the moment, in no hurry to get to the next moment, whatever that moment might bring.

On the last morning of vacation, a bright, sunny morning not unlike this morning on the San Andreas Trail, we started out early to do what we could before the midday sun shut us down. We were heading toward the Oltra Arno to see a man named Francesco who made hand-sewn leather shoes in a small shop with a red door. We had visited him the day before, had stepped into the one-room shop and become intoxicated, liquored up, by the smell of shoe leather and polish. His wife, Anna, made the sale. She didn't smile once while I was deciding between the leather slip-on or the sandal until I put the plastic down and then she showed me her teeth and pointed to her breasts, shouting, "Io, Anna."

I *Io*-ed my name back and made plans to return the next day to pick up the shoes, which Francesco was altering a millimeter for a perfect fit.

We walked over the bridge, the Ponte Santa Trinita, which crosses the Arno not far from the famous fourteenth-century bridge, the Ponte Vecchio. I looked down into the water as I imagined countless others had done, as people for centuries have looked down into the Seine or the Danube, to see their reflection or light on the water, to somehow cement the moment in memory. There I saw what I least expected to find, something I have always feared. For some people it's birds, some snakes. Shots can handle anything with four or less legs but falls apart when it comes to millipedes. She says it's all those tiny, tiny feet. (Suggesting what? Trampling? Scuff marks?) I'm sure studies have been done about which creatures' signal what kind of terror in which type of individual, but all I knew was that this thing in the water was my waterloo, my Freddy Krueger, my No. 1 candidate.

It was large (larger than most), furry (furrier than most), with a tail as long as a ruler. To make my fear understandable there is personal history that must be dredged up. (If they dredged the Arno what history would surface in the detritus found? Ancient Etruscan clay pots or sixteenth-century codpieces? World Wars One and Two memorabilia? Italian designer wear from the 1970s, a platform high heel cast off in a moment of abandon?) Rodents have haunted my dreams since childhood, when my fisherman father would take me down to the docks at night to check on his boat. Scampering across the dock planks were wharf rats, the largest rodents in the world, comparable to the Norway rat, or "Old World" rat, *Rattus norvegicus*, with its grayish-brown body with whitish underparts and a long, scaly tail. I remember one wharf rat running by as the head-lights of the Jeep shot out at him. He stopped, turned and looked at us with iridescent green eyes. I remember the color most distinctly.

I was never quite the same after that. My childhood fear carried through my teen years and into adulthood, growing in significance—as our fears often do. If anyone uses the "R-word" in polite conversation, I have an antidote. Under my breath, I say "rats, rats, rats," then cough or clear my throat. In doing so I bring the image to consciousness, as a precautionary measure, because then the thing itself will not enter my subconscious and return to visit in dreams. Haven't you noticed that if you think, only for an instant, of someone during the daytime or glimpse someone out of the corner of your eye, it's as if they haven't been given their proper due? They come back at night with a vengeance, as rats did, gargantuan rats, colossal rats, skyscraper rats, who inhabited my dreams for years until I found this cure.

The Arno, the color of its water now brownish, muddy, already altered, was never again to be a river of romantic associations. The creature went swimming by and, as I was in Florence, my associative process went something like this: Italy, European cities with waterways, Venice, canals, Thomas Mann's *Death in Venice*, the film version with Dirk Bogarde in a white summer linen suit and that scene of many R's scurrying about, carrying their special delivery letters to the people next door. Then my mind went to the Middle Ages, then the Plague. I began thinking about what carried the disease, and thought that the modern-day Florentines are cruising for a bruising if they have creatures this large swimming about, and—well—couldn't history repeat itself, as it often does, as sometimes a moment repeats itself again and again?

Shots saw my reaction, looked down and saw the thing in the water. She's heard me murmur "rats, rats, rats" at dinner parties, at family reunions, and has always quickly changed the topic of the conversation so people won't notice my ritual. I must have covered my eyes and trembled, because an Italian man who stood fifteen feet from us, who was also gazing into the water, began to laugh and shake his head back and forth and shout "No, no, no."

He rifled off a string of Italian words in rapid-fire delivery and when I shouted back, "No capito," he said a word I did not comprehend but that sounded like "Nivea," my favorite hand cream.

Shots, who knows some Italian, went over and spoke with him and then returned and translated his message. He said it wasn't an R-word but instead a harmless, benign mammal called a nutria that belonged to the otter family. I looked again and, sure enough, the creature was floating on its back, cupping something to its chest, acting like a California otter with abalone shell in one hand and a rock in the other, cracking something open for dinner. I looked again and tried to make the R-word and the nutria kissing cousins, but try as I might I could not get the Plague out of my head—bodies were floating everywhere—so we politely said our "grazie" and went on our way.

As we approached the crest of the bridge, the midpoint, everyone around us was looking up in the sky. A street sweeper, who, by the very nature of his work usually looks down, shielded his eyes and looked up, toward the east. A group of schoolchildren pointed up, up. We looked toward the ball of sun rising over the city and there, partially blocking the sun, like an eclipse, we saw something as large, as out of place, as incongruous as a California otter would be in the Arno.

A hot air balloon has always brought to mind another time, not here, not now, but somewhere near the turn of the nineteenth century. Perhaps one of the draws then (and now, in California, where the balloons fill the sky above the vineyards) was the sense that you could float your cares away and, at the same time, get from point A to point B (but given that the balloon's aim was less accurate, maybe point F, maybe in the general vicinity of Y). While I could picture a hot air balloon in Napa or Kansas or the Emerald City, it was harder to picture one in Italy. Yet, here was such a balloon, floating above the Arno, bringing to the morning the nineteenth century's slower sense of time—as if the Italians needed any more reason to decrease the pace.

That, in and of itself, would have been a moment, wouldn't it? But there were extenuating circumstances that heightened the moment, that made it something more than what it was. The balloon was in trouble. The balloon was going down, not up, was descending, a few feet every minute, was staggering (if balloons indeed stagger) in an uncontrollable manner. It was hard to imagine this was its intention, to head towards the river, but there it was, heading down the down escalator, losing ground. As the balloon lost altitude I could make out three people in the basket: a youngish blonde-haired woman, a youngish brown-haired man, and an older bald man in a yellow sport shirt, frantically working the controls. I could see the sputtering blue flame filling the balloon with hot air to keep it aloft. But something was terribly wrong. Between one ponte and the next, this hot air balloon was heading towards the Arno.

On the sidelines the crowd was hoping for lift. I felt the people around us rooting for the balloon. We all stood at the middle of the bridge and as the balloon careened toward us, I could make out some script painted across its girth, some form of writing. There was red lettering on the yellow background. What I initially read as PIAZZA RUSSARE— Snore Square—which made no sense, turned into PIZZA RUNNER, which made no sense. There was a graphic of a rabbit carrying a pizza box, speeding along, something the balloon wasn't doing. Why choose such a languid vehicle to communicate speed? I was surprised the script was in English, not Italian, and wondered who the target audience was. But I couldn't stay in this reverie, which would require time, which is what reveries require, slow, ambling, non-digital time, for then the rabbit and all descended too far. The balloon dived; the basket and its inhabitants hit the waters of the Arno and, by association, the waters of the nutria. The bottom of the basket bounced as it hit, skimmed the surface, and then, divine fortune, there was one last burst of flame, and the balloon gave a little rabbit hop, its final burst of enthusiasm. The basket touched but did not sink, and the balloon, like an indecisive soufflé, momentarily rose again.

But where could the balloon rise to, and how fast? Coming up quickly was the next bridge. Unless there was a great updraft, the basket was set to crash into the fourteenth-century bridge embankment. We were bracing for catastrophe, for a collision. Wasn't this exactly what we were experiencing? Was this not a collision of time zones, of centuries? Here we were, standing above the plague-ridden waters of the fifteenth century, while all around us rose the architecture of thirteenth- and fourteenth-century Florence, and here, too, a hot air balloon of the nineteenth century covered with twenty-first-century advertising. So many centuries were in this moment! There was no separation! It was as if we were standing on the fault line of history, the fault line that divides one century from the next, one moment from the next. Here we were at the moment the world broke open, when the earth opened up.

Were all moments a series of connected associations from other times? How could one be in the moment when crowding in were a host of associations and memories and architectures and messages from the past? There was no separation between this moment and that, between the present and the past, between this era and the one that came before—or perhaps even the one that comes after. Who knows what will happen next, what insurmountable mystery or collision or catastrophe awaits just around the next corner? What nirvana right around the next bend? How can you prepare for any of it? While we may take comfort in the fact that we have our earthquake kit stocked and ready at home, isn't preparedness beyond the point? Was this what the Buddhist nun was getting at?

The basket did hit the embankment. It stopped and could go no farther. The people inside the basket swayed for a moment. The balloon billowed over the bridge, but the traffic, like time, did not stop. Scooters beeped and small cars hummed as if to say "Andiamo." *Let's go.*

Some people standing on the bridge quickly grabbed the guide ropes that hung down from the side of basket, grabbed hold, as if seizing an idea, carefully pulled up the basket so that it was parallel to the bridge surface, and held it there. The basket's occupants disembarked to wild applause. There was much yelling and Italian-style chaos. A van arrived with a Pizza Runner logo and deposited a troop of frantic ad execs.

Shots and I waited and watched, but it looked as though the rescue effort was going to take a long time, a very, very long time, and this was the last day of vacation and our time was limited. So we went on our way to see Francesco about the shoes.

$$\text{⚓} \quad \text{⚓} \quad \text{⚓}$$

My morning walk was almost over. What had I missed on the trail? I was out of this moment, out of time, thinking, ironically, of another moment in which I was fully present. On the San Andreas Trail, I was trying, without success, to stay in the moment but there, in Italy, I was thrust into the moment, no choice involved, and no effort required, effortlessly cast in the sea of history and time. Do we simply not have to try so hard? My sunscreen is wearing off, the topical application is thinning. Maybe the moment is all the time we have. Maybe that is all the time in the world.

When I returned from Italy I looked up the definition of nutria in the dictionary. It didn't say otter, but sent me to "coypu." And under coypu? "A large South American aquatic rodent, yielding the fur nutria."

I certainly couldn't go back and find the man and make my point, and what was the point anyway? In front of me, on the San Andreas Trail, the world can break open at a moment's notice. I have a ringside seat on upheaval. There, up ahead on the path, is a California gray squirrel, a furry creature—while not ratlike, somewhat coypu-like—with a long, albeit bushy, tail. The squirrel goes scurrying by, swimming by, negotiating the cracks in the path as it carries its message into the next moment and the next.

Time Trials at the Labyrinth

I DROP MY COINS INTO THE PARKING METER ON HYDE STREET, realize I have a good half-hour before my doctor's appointment, where she'll check my blood pressure, cholesterol, will prescribe a remedy or set me free. I decide to put the time to good use, get a little cardio in, so I walk down Hyde, past a secondhand store with a faded copy of a Michael Crichton's book in the window, past a series of flea bag hotels. I let the WALK DON'T WALK signs lead me, remember a line from a book by Joan Didion, "when all the lights turned green for me," written long before her personal tragedies, when all the lights turned red for her, as they have for the man sitting on the curb with his head in his hands. What's his story?

I don't stop. I pick up the pace, shift direction, go up Taylor, the SROs (single-room occupancy hotels) giving way to many-room occupancy buildings, a brass banister here, a stained-glass window there, and then, rising up like a gray iceberg, Grace Cathedral. I'd been inside once, years ago, to hear an evening of Gregorian chant, but since then the Labyrinth has been installed, a circular maze, a meditation zone, that allows a person to walk in silence, to calm down, which is what I need, given the blood pressure cuff headed my way. Maybe I can even lower my cholesterol without Lipitor?

I step inside, head toward the back of the church where I find a circle with curving paths inside, embossed on a grayish carpet. I didn't know there was an interior version. I speedread a sign, TAKE OFF YOUR SHOES, which I do, and then, to the sound of some internal starting gun, I begin to walk.

Happily, I am alone. If there were slow-goers ahead I'd have to ask to play through. Though I don't play golf, I don't usually find myself on labyrinths either.

There are a few tourist types inside the church, maybe hoping for a sighting of the celebrities who are known to frequent Grace. (Did they have an opening night gala for the Labyrinth? Did Sharon Stone walk the gray carpet?) No one's looking my way, so I walk at a brisk pace, a short length, then turn as the path turns, a tight hairpin. When I shift direction there is the smallest hesitation, I have to almost stop. On the next length I do a slow jog, trying to make up for lost time.

I start to wonder if with these shifts, these quick turns, there is a corresponding turn of thought. With each turn of a story do we change direction? Shots, who works as a nurse practitioner at the county hospital, has a theory. People get a free pass the first two turns of their story. They get the benefit of the doubt. But if the explanation for why they missed an appointment or didn't take their meds goes past two turns, well, something's up. And with another turn in the labyrinth I start thinking about the man who came to the door last night, who knocked after lights-out, which in our house is early, before nine p.m.—before *CSI* or *Cold Case*, all those crime shows with dead bodies and autopsies that are supposed to put you in the mood for a little shut-eye.

I opened the door, even though I know better. There he stood, six feet tall, a hooded sweatshirt, a day's stubble on pale skin, hands in his jeans. "Ma'am," he said, "my car broke down. Can you help me out with a little cash?"

I start to say no, not tonight, when he says, "I had to pull off the freeway. My little girl is in the car." And I picture the little girl, locked inside. Did he leave the window open? When I look concerned, he says, "She's very sick, I was taking her to the hospital," and I think, *God, what if it's true? Let's call 911.* I turn to reach for my wallet, the phone, and then, with the smallest hesitation, he says, "I stopped by the bank machine to get some cash but it ate my card," and quickly, "See, I was mugged yesterday," then the picture of the girl goes out the window, as does the car, the bank card, for it's not one, not two, but five turns of story. I just don't think I can go the distance.

A trio of out-of-towners stands outside the circle, whispering to each other. Do they want to get on? I look down at my watch, I'm off my pace, but my thoughts are speeding. I turn again, head towards the center, towards the heart of the matter. Why shouldn't I think the best of my fellow man or woman? Which way should I turn, towards belief or cynicism? How many turns does it take to convince a person of your story and what if your life really has spun out of control, like I'm spinning here, like Didion's spun when her husband and daughter died in one year's time? How do you walk a labyrinth when you have lost all sense of direction?

I'm sweating now, the tourists are looking my way, so I sprint to the finish, round the last turn, running for my life. I reach the center, check my heart rate which is way up, pump my fist in the air like Tiger Woods, like I've made a hole in one. *Yes,* I say silently, *oh yes.* A guy in plaid Bermudas walks over.

"Ma'am," he says, "What's the point of going around a circle? If I'm here," he steps into the circle's opening, "and there's where I want to be," he points to the clover center, "why not just step over the lanes? Why not cut to the chase?"

I start to tell him why I walk-ran the whole thing, about my doctor's appointment, the cardio workout, the man at the door, how I've never golfed, how all this relates to heart health, and then I see him slowly back away.

Five turns.

Lambs of God and the New Math

SHOTS AND I ARE JUNKIES FOR THE MIRACULOUS. WE SEEK OUT testimonies from the faithful about spontaneous healings, hunt for lucky charms, carry back magical dirt from an adobe church in Chimayo, New Mexico, that causes the infirm to cast off their crutches and walk again. Last year, when it was reported that at a local cemetery the image of Our Lady of Guadalupe appeared on a sawed-off tree limb—formed by mold and fungus—we knew we had to go. Along with hundreds of followers, we made the pilgrimage every day and watched as people left flowers, prayer cards, dollar bills, and my favorite: a Reese's Peanut Butter Cup wrapper tacked to the tree, someone's most cherished item. It's clear each person wanted something miraculous to occur in their lives, freedom from sickness, from money woes, from awful in-laws. Everyone wanted to get out from under. We kept going each day until microbiology triumphed. The mold turned into more mold and finally, one day, the Virgin's face disappeared.

Maybe our desire to witness miracles all started when, like many of our middle-aged friends, we began looking for meaning in our lives. Shots started reading about the medieval women saints who went through all kinds of hell and back to experience transcendence. We traveled to Italy two summers ago to see the ultimate relic, the head of Saint Catherine of Siena on display in the Basilica di Santo Domenico. Thousands make the pilgrimage yearly. For a few lira, the altar where she is housed lights up, and her head—a mummified skull dressed in a white nun's habit, "dressed" as if she were on her way to lauds—takes on an electric glow.

The story goes that after a short life of performing miracles, Saint Catherine died of the illness that would, years later, befall Karen Carpenter: anorexia nervosa. She was buried but wasn't allowed to rest for long. In hopes her daughter would win designation as an incorruptible, Catherine's mother let the church exhume the corpse to prove Catherine's body had not decayed. (I can only wonder about that mother-daughter dynamic.) She then promptly gave Catherine's head to the church in Siena and her body to Rome. Shots always says that Saint Catherine is the original poster girl for the mind-body split.

So when we heard the relics of Saint Thérèse of Lisieux were going to be on display in the Bay Area we decided to make the journey to see them. Saint Thérèse, the saint they call "the little flower," spent her life always doing good and taught a simple way of confidence in God without limits. She died in 1897, and now, over a century later, the church was taking her bones around the world in a little box for the faithful to see. When living she was reported to have said, "I would like to preach the Gospel on all five continents—until the consummation of the ages." Posthumously, they were giving her her wish. Post-grave, she was getting the grand tour.

On the day of the event Shots and I rise early and drive up to Napa, a drive that takes us past spring-green farmlands and new-growth vineyards. The spindly arms of each new grapevine branch out along the fence wires and look like the body of Christ on the cross—if you are in a spiritually associative frame of mind. Once we enter the city limits, we follow our map and drive to the middle of town, where we find the Church of St. John the Baptist. I'm disappointed to see it is one of those monolithic church structures built to give the visual impression of a modern-day ark, a tall ship of a building rising to four square peaks. From a distance the roof looks like a giant washing-machine agitator.

Inside the church, everything is a little too cheery. Banners hang from the ceiling, heralding this and that. The sun filters in through modern stained-glass windows, depicting of the Stations of the Cross in vivid primary colors. The church architects seemed bent on stripping the space of any hint of darkness or mystery or blood on the cross, any suggestion that the trip over the River Styx was anything deeper and darker than a Disneyland ride.

The place is packed, so we find a pew in one of the side alcoves, behind a group of elders, their gray heads bent in prayer. Some folksy guitar music is playing—New Vatican meets Peter, Paul and Mary (before Peter was arrested for child molestation.) On cue, the small children from the Catholic school file in wearing the officially sanctioned uniforms, bright red cardigan sweaters over white shirts or blouses and dark pants or skirts. On their heels come the true believers, the church's established status quo, their necks bowed low to suggest the proper supplicant position.

The priest, a portly fellow in a cream-colored gown, appears from a secret side panel in the back of the church. He takes his place in front of the altar on the circular stage, a theater-in-the-round design to promote the new intimacy. It's soon apparent the purpose for this address is to give us all a little instruction before the festivities begin.

"This is a glorious opportunity for all of us to reflect on the goodness of Saint Thérèse of Lisieux. We are truly blessed to have her visit." He directs his initial comments toward the schoolchildren. There is something punitive in his tone of voice, a drill-sergeant delivery he's using to enforce the reverential, just in case reverence isn't springing naturally from within. He wants to impress upon the teenagers that this is as big a deal as, say, 'N Sync come to call, or for the younger children, as cool an event as meeting a Power Ranger.

The priest shifts his focus and addresses the rest of us. "As there are so many of you, please, once you reach the relic, do not kneel and tarry. We're on a tight schedule today and this will slow the line. Please say your prayers and intentions on approach," he says, as if we are little planes lined up in the spiritual skies above SFO, wheels down, in a holding pattern.

I whisper to Shots, "What a great idea! Express Prayer. Maybe we can get a cappuccino to go," and she tells me to shush, which draws a stern look from an old lady with a crucifix the size of a butter knife hanging upon her chest. When I look up I see people are already readying their thoughts and prayers, prioritizing, holding on to some intentions, turfing others, deciding which are nonessential prayers (getting a word in for Uncle Bill and his battle with gout, the prayer for a new powerboat) given the new limitations.

When everyone is seated the pomp and circumstance begins. The Knights of Columbus enter, six very old men dressed in red velveteen capes, swords drawn, *HMS Pinafore* caps on their heads. The swords are at the ready just in case someone bursts in and what? Makes a heist? Are there pirates who deal in the relic trade? The altar boys and girls, then the priests and their various sidekicks follow the Knights, then, finally, Saint Thérèse.

When the little box comes into view it is different than I imagined. I knew we wouldn't see the bones, but I expected to see a relic of a container that suggested its own kind of mystery, perhaps an old wooden box battered in its transcontinental shufflings. Instead, a second contingent of Knights carry a small ornate building covered in gold filigree, a mini architectural wonder that looks like a miniature Versailles, with grand columns and cornices. It's as elaborate as a rich child's dollhouse that's been detailed right down to the main ballroom's itsy chandelier.

The small building sits under a large plastic dome, which covers the whole thing like a football stadium Super Dome or a bell jar that covers an antique clock. (I once knew a man who worked at the AIDS ward at SF General Hospital who, after a visit from Elizabeth Taylor, grabbed her Styrofoam coffee cup from the desk, with the half arc of her lipstick blotted on the rim, and had it ensconced under a glass dome for perpetuity.) The truth is, this dome isn't made of glass, which has some physical integrity, but is Plexiglas, which seems to cheapen the experience. The faithful must touch the Plexiglas that covers the box that covers the relic, somewhere deep inside, where a bone or two of Thérèse's lie.

When I whisper to Shots that this wasn't what I hoped for, she quietly explains the mathematics of the church, how religious power and meaning becomes an equation. "A relic is a part of a person or a thing, a fragment of the true cross, or a fragment of a bone," she says. "A secondary relic is that which the original relic resides in or touches, like when a piece of cloth touched the true cross or bone. A tertiary relic has touched something that's touched something. With each touch, each removal, there is an exponential decrease in power."

Based on this system, the plastic dome is a tertiary relic, three times removed from the original article, and removed from anything real is what I'm feeling at the present moment. I find all this as difficult to comprehend as the new math. If an object's power dilutes—like a weakened brew—the farther away you are from the object, does meaning dilute as well? Or what if instead there's an inverse relationship? What if the object's power becomes stronger, fueled by hope and imagination to even greater meaning?

There must be a sign I don't pick up on, a silent trumpet call heard by the pure of heart that signals it's time to honor the relic, for suddenly there's lots of movement, people shuffling about, adjusting their collars, straightening their clothes, putting themselves in order as if they're about to be on view. First the children file forth, which is to be expected, as they are closer to holiness than we will ever be. They have yet to become embittered or cynical, haven't developed the capacity for making bad cappuccino jokes about a holy procession. Then, in march more of the faithful, people with special dibs, powerful people in the church. The rest of the crowd, which is sizeable, is instructed to file afterward, row by row.

When it finally comes time for our pew to go, we first walk single file down the side aisles of the church and then make a U-turn to march down the center aisle. Given the length of the line, there is lots of time to pre-pray.

Shots gives me a religious medal and a Kleenex to wipe across the dome, since somehow she still believes—though she has been through Buddhism, atheism, pantheism, and animism and has not as yet come to any definite conclusions. There must still be a crumb, a shred of the original Catholic belief lodged in her from her twelve years in Catholic schools. Some slim belief still resides in some part of her, under the stairway of the spine or in a secret alcove in the body, an elbow, a small toe. Prior to coming today she visited a religious supply store and bought the religious medal with Saint Christopher on the front and a picture highlighting modes of transportation on the back. There's a train, a boat, and a plane. All we need is Dionne Warwick's strained, high voice, and her connection to the Psychic Network to transport us away.

On approach there's a backup. People aren't following the directions. Maybe there is an anarchistic uprising of sorts; people will not be rushed with their intentions, and this cheers me. A woman up at the podium microphone recites a long oration on Saint Thérèse's life story as we wait. "She died on September 30, 1897, loving with a heart as big as the world itself." A heart so big it surely couldn't have fit in that small box we are fast approaching.

As we near the relic we can see the ones just before us: a middle-aged woman with a pronounced limp who bows down with some difficulty, places a red rose on the floor in front of the relic, and needs help to stand back up; followed by an elderly husband and wife, he with his hand protectively at the small of her back, guiding her, steering her forward. As if they have rehearsed for this at home, both, in one synchronized movement, kiss the top of the dome. Then there are some nondescript types: a man in a business suit, a woman in a pink scarf, another woman in a sweatsuit with a mantilla covering her head. I think, *My God, people need to believe.* I look skyward, up at the ceiling, and for a moment think of the lost intention of this structure, like so many of our lost intentions, barely remembered. Gothic architecture was meant to provide the high ceilings necessary to accommodate all the prayers that fill the church cavity, every wish for a connection to something larger than this life that swells in each breast and ascends, floating upwards toward the rafters, as heat rises. And maybe in each plea, each prayer in a bottle tossed out to sea, there's an unexpressed desire to go with, to follow the ones who have already departed and now only occasionally return in shards of bone. The truth of it is we are all here, every one of us, on the off chance these bones can bring some word back from the other side. Maybe word from our own dearly departed or from those we only hear about in the news: the young men lost to gang warfare, the women who trusted a stranger, the elderly who answered the doorbell and let the "nice man" in, and so many more.

I watch a young man two people up from us who looks oddly out of place. He is wearing dirty, faded jeans and a black Raiders jacket and has his cap pulled low across his brow. He looks to be about twenty-five, but it's hard to tell given his posture: his body is bent down like an old man's, hunched over, his hands stuffed deep in his jacket pockets. I can picture him at the ballpark or at the local tavern but not here, in the middle of the day, with time on his hands. When he gets close, when it's his turn, he stops in front of the relic, stands there and is unable to move. There's a nervous buzz in the line about the delay. Then, as if remembering his lost intention, he pulls two small blue knitted baby booties out of his jacket pocket, soft tiny booties, and slowly rubs the booties the length of the Plexiglas, in a loving arc, the gentlest of gestures, like when you put your hand upon a baby's face, as much to feel the softness as to shield that cheek from a world of harm. Everyone goes silent; all movement in the line stops, for it is too much, all of this is too much. We know the baby has already gone to God, made the journey, and here we are on this side, with no way to ford the distance. And there is sorrow that has no depth and prayers that have no influence and before I know it it's my turn and I rub the medal, then the Kleenex along the length of the dome, press it firmly on the Plexiglas, I shine the dome and feel something, deep and heartfelt, a small crack, an opening, and almost cry but get a grip. If this is all projection or magic, intentional or not, at this moment I don't care, and I send a prayer up to the rafters for my loved ones. I feel it ascend.

⚓   ⚓   ⚓

"We all seem to have a need to go back to our earliest beginnings," Shots says as we drive away.

I think of paleontologists, archaeology, the necessity to go on some kind of dig, and I remember a line I wrote once: *She could read scat like there was no tomorrow.* Or was it *She could sing scat like there was no tomorrow?* Which makes me think of Ella, as holy as they come, closer to God than any priest in the church we've just left behind.

Shots continues, "We never seem to lose the desire. There's a need to connect to the unknown, and maybe, when we were very, very young, maybe we felt—and were—more connected. Remember when we were small, how everything was large, landscapes were large, feelings were large, before memory interceded, before we ascribed things meaning? There weren't the layers of reasoning and analysis to get through. Remember when, as a kid, you would lie flat on your back in the grass and look up and you fell into the clouds or the intense blue of the sky? Or the first time your toes touched the lake's edge and the jolt was electric? There wasn't any distance between you and the world. Nothing got in the way."

It's true. I know so many friends who have taken treks to the places they inhabited as children, homeward-bound journeys to see the site of the early "miracles." But the places are never the same. Shots grew up in a little corner store in Louisville, Kentucky, Faust's Market, her father's place. I've seen pictures of it over the years, the small storefront windows advertising Nehi sodas and Meadow Gold ice cream, the striped awnings, the roof banner that read QUALITY MEATS—FOOD. The store looked like a Walker Evans photograph, a place that functioned as a way station, meeting place, counseling center, along with providing everyone's daily goods. We returned last year to the store, now a sad, sagging building with a fake new front, now just a shell. Where once the shelves were packed with pork and beans and the scale swayed under the weight of ground round, where the bell of the screen door rang its little song and the penny candy stuck together in the glass jars, now there was nothing but batten and board.

"Take the church, for example," she continues. "When I return to the church, the place of some of my first memories, the Mass, the Latin and singing, the place seems like a husk, empty and strangely small. We go back to the place where meaning resided, but where did the meaning go? We return to a place where we were first introduced to things not of this world. And yet that world has changed beyond recognition."

We drive in silence after that. Before long we leave any semblance of city behind and farm fields appear with horses, then sheep. A long stretch of asphalt lies before us and we speed in an effort to get somewhere, to leave our disappointments behind. The highway is a gray ribbon that cuts through the center of the green hills and I notice that a car up ahead of us suddenly makes a sharp turn and swerves over to the side of the road. We slow down and I spot an arm reaching outside the passenger side window, as if signaling to us, pointing to the fields.

We see what they see: new lambs, just born, some barely standing on their new limbs, others racing in circles, kicking it up. Little black lambs and white ones frolicking—the word must have been invented for newborn lambs—and I say, "Oh, Jesus, stop, stop," and Shots shouts, "Lambs of God, lambs of God," for if there is a divine hand it has been hard at work creating this scene.

"There's not a calculating bone in their bodies," Shots says, an odd comment, but true. We get out of the car, stand and watch, then ascribe human qualities to the lambs—they are guileless, innocent, generous in their play. We stay there and the wonder of this vision grows as surely as the vines are growing. Why would we find what we were looking for here, out in the open, a connection to something larger, to meaning, when we've just left the church, the designated place where meaning was supposed to reside? These lambs—removed from the logic and mathematics of the church, are as close to a real God as we'll ever get. Out here, nothing signals the arrival of wonder, no trumpet or ceremony, no official designation of this field as saintly or pure. Yet here is the unknown, the unexpected, and we can't help but be altered from who we were a moment ago.

As we leave I glance back at the scene. If I widen my view the green rolling fields are active, fluid, and look like the sea. The lambs bob and crest, swimming in the bright green waves, their heads like little white-caps, and happiness floods in like water through a busted pipe. Like Saint Thérèse, we're released from all that once confined us and we are on the ocean, traveling the world again.

The Windy City

WHEN THE AIRPORT SCREENER AT O'HARE ASKS TO LOOK IN my suitcases I smile my most trustworthy smile. *I'm a lamb*, says the smile, *I am an innocent.*

I am security, he smiles back. I know he is going to have to check.

I have nothing to hide so I stand back as he opens my suitcase and reaches in. He feels here, feels there, manhandles my vacation togs, my sunny outfits, my swimsuit, my pjs, my fragile underthings. When his face clouds over I can tell he's come across something hard, unyielding. He pulls out my red Swiss Army knife, the one item of sentimental value, the gift Shots gave me on our fifth anniversary. The knife has useful attachments; three blades, a screwdriver, a plastic toothpick, a fish-scaler, all of which are—now that I think about it—pointed and dangerous, yet necessary for the trout I plan to catch, the wooden toys I plan to whittle, the tooth decay I plan to prevent.

I tell him I forgot, momentarily, about the terror, the color-coded alerts, the random acts of violence. I tell him I forgot that sharp equals bad. He dives back in and finds my Louis Vuitton makeup bag, (all right, the knock-off Vuitton bag, but can he tell? Is artifice a new crime on Homeland Security's ever-growing list?) He unzips the knock-off zipper and finds my tweezers, eyelash curler, the small sharp scissors for trimming unwanted facial hair (or, might he think, to alter a disguise?) so unlike the dull paper scissors we used to make cutouts in kindergarten.

He puts the knife and the make up bag in the takeaway bin. I know he would let me pass if not for the corkscrew he finds in the side pocket of the carryall. I tell him that I believe in preparedness, too. I wanted to be prepared for room service, a bottle of red, a rib-eye steak.

Attached as I am to the knife, the tweezers, the corkscrew, I know these are just things; they are material, expendable. I could, if push comes to shove, let them go, for, when you think about it, isn't that what vacation is about, letting go, leaving worry behind? But a worried look is what he gives me when he reaches the bottom of the bag and comes upon the acupuncture needles. I threw them in at the last minute, innocent health boosters, but I can tell he sees them as pointed, deadly weapons, packaged like little swords in their individual plastic sheaths.

"Hey, guys, get a load of this," the screener yells to the rest of security, and three burly men come over from their stations and gaze into the palm of his hand as if reading a very bad fortune.

There are long needles for shoulders and back, short needles for head and neck. There are needles that, once in, will open up what in acupuncture lingo are called the "four gates," the "points of joy," the "windows of the sky." The men look at the little mountain of needles as they might gaze at the mountains of Nepal, as if they are that remote. They stare at me as if I am that remote.

I need an alibi, a cover. I am a part-time acupuncturist, I tell them—a lie, but Shots is, they are her needles, and she's taught me some tricks. I was planning to give myself a treatment on vacation, as a way to relax, but when they ask to see my California ID again I know I'm getting the treatment now. The photo was taken ages ago. I looked so different then, with the big square glasses, with my hair slicked back, like Angela Davis on the run. I unclench my raised fist to make them feel more comfortable, and when that doesn't work I fall back on my wiles. I plead, "I am sorry, I'll never pass this way again, I'll never return to Chicago."

I see them weaken, and I would have them in the palm of my hand except that my screener decides to be safe, to make one final pass through my bags. Under the running shoes, under the sarong, he finds the hidden weapon—a lumpy bundle of fabric, a thick roll of red, blue, and yellow squares. The color-coded squares alert him that he's on to something. I explain that they are Tibetan prayer flags. Each individual flag has a printed prayer, and I pictured attaching the bunch to palm trees, then letting the island winds blow. As I sip my tropical drink the winds will distribute the prayers—with very little effort on my part—prayers for world peace, for understanding. The flags are attached, on a line, like cutouts, I tell him, like paper dolls made in kindergarten.

He holds the bundle gingerly, as if it might explode. He looks at me, then at the bundle. I smile. A smile that says *I'm sorry to have met you. I never intended you any harm.*

Then he squeezes. He squeezes the roll hard to feel for something sharp hidden in the folds. The noise of the terminal stops as if the world is holding its breath. And that's when I hear it. Faintly at first, then louder. The flags cry out. They cry out for us to give up our attachments. They cry out with eternal blessings of long life, happiness, good health, world peace. Each time he squeezes, the flags send out their prayers to the screeners, the ticket takers, to me. They cry out and, blown by the winds of this windy city, they bless all of our shining little heads.

The Road to Shalimar

SORRY, FOLKS. FECES FOUND. THE POOL IS CLOSED UNTIL FURTHER NOTICE.

The little sign has surprising power. Enough to stop my vacation ritual. Every afternoon, at exactly five-thirty, during the quietest part of the day, I sneak down the stairs of the seaside hotel to go swimming. Before the sun is over the yardarm, as a Southern friend says, when the hot sun of the Outer Banks of North Carolina in late June lessens just a bit. For a half-hour I take a few laps in peace while the families are in their bungalows having dinner. I picture them serving up their vacation meals, something easy and short on preparation like hot dogs or pizza or takeout from Mama Dip's barbecue. Nothing that requires the time it would take to prepare a real Southern meal like Country Captain or Brunswick Stew, where everything goes into the mix, leftover chicken, beef, bacon. Even a squirrel if you have one handy.

All day long, from the shade of our hotel balcony, I watch the children commandeer the pool. I watch their bobbing little forms. They scream. They shout. They churn. The waters churn. Without the visual it sounds like an audience of five-year-olds watching a horror flick.

Post signage, the pool is a flat, calm, turquoise square. I consider my options. I could walk the fifty steps it takes to reach the Atlantic Ocean, that warm pool of a sea just beyond the rise of sand and boardwalk. (The ocean here flows like a river, left to right, not east to west or out to in like the Pacific, where Shots and I live, where the ocean comes straight at you.) Or I can walk out to Cape Hatteras to take pictures of the non-operational lighthouse with its famous barber pole stripes halted mid-swirl.

Last evening, in the fading summer light, Shots and I stood in the shadow of the monument and watched as tourists posed for photos in front of the CLOSED FOR REPAIRS sign. A young girl, not more than sixteen, sauntered up. She had three little children in tow, another bun in the oven. The father, no more than a boy himself, followed behind. He wore cutoffs and was shirtless, revealing a small sunken chest. As he walked, the camera around his neck swung out and in, landing right in the middle of his breastbone, leaving a dent with each hit, like the dings you see in car doors. As mother and children were positioning themselves in front of the guardrail around the lighthouse, I heard the father repeat, "Dakota,

Sierra, Michelle. Stand next to your mama, look at your daddy. Stand next to your mama, look at your daddy." With his Southern accent the directions sounded soft and melodic, like a rhythmic lullaby.

I decide to return to the balcony and continue reading the book I've left face down on my balcony chair. I am in the South for the first time, the home of all that great Southern literature, and one of the designated tasks I've given myself on this trip is to read the entire short story collection of the Southern writer Eudora Welty. Every story, front to back. I want to savor the lines, listen closely to her mastery of dialogue on the page, then hear the voices spoken in the air and receive that immediate aural gratification. Ever since I got off the plane in Durham it felt like I landed on a huge sound set. At gas stations, on the radio, at the hotel lobby, the voices sang out to create a new musical score: *Stand Next to Your Mama. Look at Your Daddy.*

One of my reasons for traveling here was to be introduced to the South I've read about for so many years. Another was to visit the part of the country where Shots grew up, its culture unfamiliar to me. Having lived my entire life on the West Coast, I know only of its migratory populations, all the loose marbles that roll to that side of the map. Here we are, finally, on the other side of the board game of America.

There had been another reason to travel. Both of us are past due for a vacation. We need to cut loose the tethers of our lives back home, all the daily encounters, the cares, the taut lines of responsibility that secure our days. We want to be free of the morning nod to the neighbor gunning his Monster Truck, free of the need to jockey for position approaching the freeway on-ramp. We want to be in a place where it doesn't matter who is ahead, a place where we can just let the other guy pass. We both work at urban epicenters—San Francisco General Hospital and SF State—where words such as "prioritize" and "triage" and "next, next, next," pepper our vocabularies. We are going on our annual vacation in hopes that we'll learn to slow down and—on a deeper, unacknowledged level, something we won't admit to each other—we hope our lives will change.

The Welty story I was reading when the pool closed down, "The Key," is about a deaf couple on their way to Niagara Falls and their chance encounter with a young man in the train station. It is the type of story that only Eudora seems capable of writing, a story about a pair of outsiders told as if she had gained access to their world, as if she were *inside* the outsiders. The Cliff Notes version of the story would read as follows: The husband wants to go to Niagara Falls, believes if they travel there their lives will change. Life from then after will be different. To take the trip will alter their patterns, their rituals and routines, their ways of being.

Isn't that what we want when we travel, a change, no matter how much we love our lives? Something to happen that will knock us off our schedules, ruled as we are by the cell, the email, the incessant stirrings and ringing of modern life?

"The Key" is a good story, and I've left it half finished. So I return to the balcony. I sit in the requisite Adirondack chair and read. Shots sits in her Adirondack chair and reads. We are well aware we are not in the Adirondacks. She's halfway through Michael Chabon's *Kavalier and Clay* when I tell her to stop reading to listen to a passage from the Welty story that points to the heart of the piece:

> [H]e became quite frightened to think that if they hadn't missed the train they would be hearing, at this very moment, Niagara Falls. Perhaps they would be standing there together, pressed against the little rail, pressed against each other, with their lives being poured through them, changing. . . .

I read it out loud. Twice. I love the idea of the little rail, imagine a guardrail put up there, on the edge of the precipice, to prevent someone from succumbing to the desire to leave all care behind, to leap into the Falls sans barrel. To throw it all away. Niagara might inspire such an action.

Shots nods and says she thinks the quote is sweet. "Sweet" is a nice word to rest on after a day of feces.

I close my eyes and listen as the ocean makes a whooshing sound like wind through a tunnel. I could fall away into this sound, fall over the edge of consciousness into daydream, then sleep, and fulfill another vacation requisite: the dead-to-the-world afternoon nap.

A child's blood-curdling scream breaks the sound barrier, as if the shark in *Jaws* just reared up in the shallow end. The pool must have opened again.

⚓   ⚓   ⚓

The next day Shots and I arise at dawn and take the ferry out to Ocracoke Island. From a trailer in the parking lot of the ferry building we buy four country ham biscuits and two Diet Pepsis. It is one of the best meals I've ever had. Washing down the biscuits with the Pepsi, I remember that Flannery O'Connor once described a character by writing that her hair dribbled down her forehead like ham gravy.

On the way back from the island we decide to buy some fish, another task to give the long sunny day some structure. The fish, with its Omega-3, will counteract the biscuits. We spot a road sign WE GOT OUR CRABS AT DIRTY DICK'S, but continue on until I spy a less provocative fish market, a two-story place that looks like a home business. Written below the WAVES SEAFOOD logo is a quote: "To everything there is a season."

I don't know how to interpret this. Is the seafood seasonal? That the previous lyric—"Turn, turn, turn"—from the old folk song, is instructive and somehow applies to the fish on display?

Shots opens the front door and we walk into a cool green room. The owners, seated behind the front counter, appear to be slow-moving, easy-going fishmongers. Glenna, of retirement age, has a golden halo of hair and a Southern accent. Levon, of retirement age, has no halo, no hair, and a Southern accent. To the right of the counter are long freezer cases where the catch of the day is arranged on the trays of ice: mahimahi, Atlantic salmon, soft-shell crab, scallops. Small white plastic tubs hold a bright red substance advertised as homemade cocktail sauce with a kick.

I notice that behind the cash register, sitting regally on a purple cushion, is a very large dog. A boxer.

"That's Hoss," Levon says. I check to see how the dog might resemble the big fella on the 1960s TV show *Bonanza*, the good-natured oafish son of Pa who never had a lot to say.

"Best dog we ever had. A real people person. Folks send pictures to him from around the world." Levon points to a bulletin board covered with snapshots of dogs frolicking under swaying palms, dogs bounding through snowdrifts. A photo of a large standard poodle with a come hither look, as sexually suggestive as any *Playboy* pinup, is signed XOXO, FROM TINY.

As if on cue, Hoss stretches up from his cushion and walks towards us. Glenna opens a swing gate between the counter and where we stand.

"Now, don't be afraid. He's real friendly. Let him shake your hand."

I'm not partial to boxers. They aren't smiley dogs. But I feel I should do the polite thing, the genteel thing, what I imagine to be the Southern thing. In a grand gesture I bend gallantly at the waist, sweep one arm out to the side, and offer my hand.

Hoss sniffs my palm. Instead of offering his paw he offers his other end. Then he lifts his leg.

I stumble backwards and land on the floor. They all fall out laughing, Glenna, Levon, Shots. Glenna can barely catch her breath but when she does she says that's Hoss's little trick. "He's never done it, I mean done it, except once. There was a lady come in and she was wearing some fancy perfume. You know, that perfume Shalimar? For some reason Hoss is wild about Shalimar. Who knew? She must have had it sprayed all up over her legs, her nylons, cause he went right over to her and watered her hose."

I can tell Glenna has worked on that hose line a long time, so I laugh. Then I look over at Hoss and wonder about the specificity of desire, what triggers what. Why Shalimar and not Emeraude or the sprightly CK1 I sprayed on this morning?

Maybe Hoss is a dog with a vivid imagination, and the word itself suggests something exotic and exciting. A place with mosques and palaces and harems. Other worlds. "Mar" as in mar of the sea. "Shali" as in shallow desire, nothing marred. There's something 1930s-sounding about the word that suggests an off-the-shoulder gown, an evening out, cocktails, seduction. Shalimar brings to mind Shangri-la, which brings to mind those old Hope and Crosby road trips. I remember the titles: *Road to Bali, Road to Morocco, Road to Zanzibar.* Was there a *Road to Shalimar*? Are we on it? Will Dorothy Lamour, scantily clad in a fetching fish apron, escape from her enforced confinement in the back room and beg to be rescued from a life of cleaning cod?

I decide it's time for the sideshow to close down. We purchase the crab, say our adieus, promise our dogs will write.

"Now you've had a taste of real Southern *Hoss*-pitality," Glenna says with all the comic timing of Bob Hope entertaining the troops.

Something about the encounter, the combination of boxers and bathroom humor and the smell of fish, has left me spinning. I need a peaceful image to end the day. On the way back to the hotel we make one last stop and turn in at the state park, where we've heard there's a turtle pond. I pull up behind a line of parked cars. A big extended family is getting out of a minivan: a mama, a papa, seven kids, from toddlers to teenagers.

Looking out over the swampy pond I see circular ripples in the water's surface. The turtles poke up their little brown heads, which look like the ends of short sticks. A young boy standing next to me cries out, "Look at their little faces, look at their faces," which, with his Southern accent, sounds like *Look at the little feces. Look at the feces.*

⚓   ⚓   ⚓

The morning sun roars up again, deep and hot. I stand at the balcony rail and look down at the scene below. The children are wild in the feces-free pool, making up for lost time.

I have moved on in the short story collection to "Why I Live at the P.O." Shots, a much speedier reader, is farther along in her book. I'm trying hard not to turn page progress into a competition.

"Hey, listen," she says.

I remind myself that this volleying, trading passages back and forth, is as much a part of a vacation as a night drive for ice cream. On vacation you can allow yourself to get untracked, to let something new in, new characters from an entirely different book into your own story. I don't see how Chabon's drama about cartoon characters is going to fit with the woman who lived at the P.O., but it's my turn to listen:

She inclined toward Joe and peered up, curving her hand around his and the flame of the match. Her eyes shone, an indeterminate color between champagne and the green of a dollar. Joe felt feverish and a little dizzy, and the cool talcum smell of Shalimar she gave off was like a guardrail he could lean against.

The guardrail again. What is it about leaning up against a guardrail that brings up such strong feelings? Why did everyone want to lean up against one? What does a guardrail guard us from or guard us against? But beyond that how can I resist the connections, the threads that are now binding all the disparate story lines together? The deaf couple, Hoss, the guardrail, and now, overlaying all of it, like a powerful cloud, the flowery, seductive scent of Shalimar?

⚓   ⚓   ⚓

The next leg of the journey takes longer then we think. There's a long, hot drive through swampland and marsh, through little towns with slant-roofed Jesus-Saves churches and barbeque chicken joints, one with a sign, CARNAL SANDERS: BREASTS, THIGHS, AND ALL THE FIXINS. Five hours into it, I need a caffeinated drink, a picker-upper. A highway sign announces that we are approaching the town of New Bern, North Carolina, the Home of Pepsi. Our closest friends back home are, at this very moment, in Bern, Switzerland, visiting their friend who is a chef for the Swiss ambassador and now has to feed Republicans.

To see the South do Bern, Switzerland, is to reel. There is a quasi-Swiss clocktower, quasi-Swiss gingerbread facades on the stores, quasi-lederhosen, and quasi-beer steins in the window displays. There are many, many banks. Outside one of the historic homes the flagpole flies the Swiss *and* Confederate flags. With this Alpine stage set I try to imagine snow covering the church spires and the branches of the mimosa trees, ice forming on the green meandering river that runs on the edge of town. Except here, the temperature is in the nineties. Maybe that's why it's the home of Pepsi: a hot place that needs a cool drink.

We stop to down a couple of sodas at a local cafe, but then Shots, in homage to her roots, orders sweet tea, a sugary tonic to beat the heat. I order a Diet Coke, realize my mistake when the waitress bangs my glass down on the counter. Here in a surreal Alpine village town with corporate allegiances I've just committed a seditious act. Across the coffee bar I hear a man whistling "Edelweiss." The world spins. Is he, too, pausing to refresh? We don't wait to find out.

By the time we reach Chapel Hill the temperature is well over one hundred degrees. We are tired, sweaty. I catch sight of the modern way station for the weary: an air-conditioned mall.

We step into Dillards, the largest department store in the complex, and walk down its cool corridors, past summer clothes, past the shoe department, past the perfume counter, when Shots suddenly stops short. I know what she's thinking.

A young man with a goatee pops up from behind the counter and asks, "May I help you?"

"Do you have Shalimar?" I ask, slightly embarrassed.

He smiles, and, after rummaging around under the counter, takes out a small spray bottle.

I spray some on my wrist. Then I do what I saw sophisticated women do as a child. I wave my wrist around in the air, an adult gesture that is as hard-wired, as scripted, as all the feminine gestures modeled by Grace Kelly or Liz or Dorothy Lamour (who would have worn something racier, like Taboo). After I wave my hand around for what I imagine is an appropriate amount of time, I lift my wrist to my nose and inhale deeply.

The scent does conjure another time and place, minarets and flowing silks and nights in the cabana. Perhaps the scent is all about losing time and place, about descending into an unfamiliar time and place that allow us to transcend our daily cares.

To hook the sale the salesman gets familiar. "Where you ladies from?"

"San Francisco." I reply, my best manners forward. "How 'bout yourself?"

"I'm from New Bern," he answers. "You know, the home of Pepsi."

Switzerland. The couple on their way to Niagara. Ham biscuits. The world spins again. How not to read significance into this? Everything is linked. Hadn't we wished to get away from the tethers? Now, here we are, players on this sound stage, our roles as scripted as Hope and Crosby's jokes. Where's the key to figuring out this drama? When can we turn the page and see how the story ends?

Quickly, I think: *WWED*. What would Eudora do?

Before any trip there are projections—of what a place will look like, of what you'll find. Before we travel we are deaf to a culture, and our assumptions guide us until something truer takes their place. I had no idea that in the South the strange would become so familiar, that events would build as poem builds, image by image, repetition by repetition. Maybe there are always other tethers, connections, stories in which we have bit parts, in places both unknown and unfamiliar.

Here we are. We are trying to hear the South, belly up to the bar, the little guardrail of the South, where there's the possibility that our lives will change, where a perfume will cause us to kick up our heels, to lift our legs.

⚓ ⚓ ⚓

A month later we are back in San Francisco, sitting down to dinner with our friends Linda and Carol, who've just come back from their European sojourn.

Over dinner they tell us about Switzerland. As we expected, the food was great. Visiting a chef is like that. During the day, when their friend was cooking, they roamed around the town and became familiar with the local customs. They take out snapshots. There's a Swiss clocktower, gingerbread houses, a large green river at the edge of town, the River Aar, the longest river in Switzerland, which takes a meander at Bern.

"People use the river as transportation," Carol says, and I look closely at one of the photographs for evidence of boats or barges or water taxis. There are some tiny round spots on the surface of the river, but nothing that looks like a vessel.

She catches my puzzled look. "No, the people *float* to work! If you look closely, you can see their little faces!"

I look again and see distinct round human spots. I can see their bobbing little forms. She points out the red handrails along the river's bank, at set intervals, like little guardrails that lead you straight into the green flowing river. The river is like a pool you can swim at any time of the day or night, open all hours, always there if you want to take a dip and float your cares away.

"Where does the river go?" I ask.

"There's a set of falls at the end. You can only go so far, or you'll go over the edge."

Like Niagara. You can only go so far. We can only go so far. After that, fate—serendipity, coincidence, call it what you will—takes over, or it doesn't. It's there around every corner, around every bend in the river, every page of the story—or it's not. Maybe if you force connection, if you go looking, the links dry up.

Linda leaves the table, then returns with a small tape recorder she's carried with her to record a soundtrack from their travels. She presses a button and we hear the shouts and cries of the daily farmer's market in Bern. Then a few bars of accordion music from street musicians. Then church bells. Then the clocktower chimes.

The next sound is unmistakable. We hear the sound of a river, a whooshing sound like wind through a tunnel, or the sound of the Atlantic from a balcony, or the sound of falls over Niagara, or the sound of a pool filter working overtime.

The Hot Spot

THREE PROP PLANES WITH DIFFERENT WING COLORS SHOW OFF their plumage: a nifty red number, an orange flitter, one with turquoise tips. We're here, at early dawn, before the skies heat up, to watch them take off into the dry air of Death Valley and toss their birdlike shadows over the Funeral Range.

As the red one starts up, its propeller blades begin to blur. "It all went by in a blur." Isn't that what people say about life? Maybe this is how the saying started, watching a propeller's quickening revolutions, the speediness with which it gains speed. It seems like only yesterday Shots and I were last standing here, on the edge of this tiny airport. In fact, it was fifteen years ago. We were both sick at the time and had traveled to the desert where, we had heard, the super-oxygenated air would have a dramatic effect on our overall sense of well-being. That was during the New Age movement, when we'd take advice like that.

Here we are again. We've decided to retrace our steps: this morning, the airstrip, later a drink at the pricey hotel up the road. Still later, a ride up to Dante's View. This is our little idea of a romantic getaway. Some go to tropical beaches, some to mountain chalets. We're going to a place where we once felt like death.

The plane just sits there, so we turn to walk back to camp. Once we turn something will happen. Something usually does when you turn away. Sure enough, behind us we hear the engine shift into a higher rev. Looking back, we see the plane taxi down the runway on its fat wheels, then lift off. There is something uplifting in seeing the plane lift up. I could stay in this moment of hopefulness except for a flitting motion at the side of the road.

A roadrunner. He sounds nothing like the cartoon character, its *beep beep* like the horn on a Karmann Ghia. There's no Wile E. Coyote in hot pursuit, though this morning we did see a pack of coyotes running across the golf course before a different pack laid claim: men in alligator-breasted shirts and khaki pants that billowed just so. There's nothing cartoonish about this bird. He seems almost debonair with his black topknot, speckled chest, and long legs like Fred Astaire. Right behind his eye there's a neon orange triangle as bright as a tiny traffic cone.

He pays us no mind. Walking down the road we shadow his movements. When he slows, we slow. When he speeds up, we speed. Without warning he veers toward the asphalt, then does what he was born to do. He runs across the road. He's true to his name, just as our bird dog points birds. He crosses over to a new set of dunes. Of course. The dunes are always sandier on the other side. We follow close behind, for there's plenty of time in Death Valley and death, we hope, is a long way off.

He walks over to a creosote bush, stops, stands still, then bends over. At his roadrunner's waist, if he had a waist. I've seen our dog do this right before she has to "bring something up." His chest swells. He bobs up and down, makes a moaning sound. Maybe it's something he ate. Suddenly there's another flash of feathers on the periphery.

"Oh, my God," Shots whispers. "It's the woman!"

There she is, less showy, in her brown plumage, Ginger Rogers running toward Fred, answering his weird mating call. She makes a beeline in his direction, then stops in the middle of the road. She bends over, pecks at something—a worm or insect?—has a quick snack, then continues. I hear him moaning. Beck and call. Or peck and call. The temperature's rising. We leave to give them privacy. As incomprehensible as their mating ritual might seem, we know that privacy is key.

⚓   ⚓   ⚓

Later that afternoon, after the drink at the hotel (where the waiter mistakes us for sisters instead of lovers) we drive up to Dante's View. In Dante's parking lot there are only a few cars. We park, then head up to a ridge where we sit and take in the panorama: the pink Panamint Mountains, Badwaters salt flats like a giant tub of milk spilled across the valley floor. In the distance, Devil's Cornfield.

I hear the sound of someone playing a guitar. Then, swelling violins. A series of flute notes. A synthesizer. An auditory mirage?

I stand up, walk to the cliff edge and look over. There, sitting below us: a young woman with blonde feathery hair, a young man staring deeply into her eyes. To their right a bottle of wine, an open picnic basket.

To their left a shiny CD player like a small spaceship, blaring out their New Age song of love. The hills are alive with the sound of music. Whether we like it or not.

I walk back and sit beside Shots. "Let's ignore them," I say. "We're here together, here again, after all these years." Then, calling up an old Monty Python line, I add, "And we're not dead yet."

I hear the screech of a hawk, but it comes from the CD, a natural sound placed there for effect.

It's a funny world. This duo set the stage then created a bubble around themselves. A romantic bell jar. With the right accoutrements their love may take flight. Oblivious, they probably can't imagine that their getaway could get in the way of our getaway. The truth is their mating ritual is as incomprehensible to us as ours might be to them. As ours was to the waiter. As Fred and Ginger's were to us. Yet all of us have something in common: we've chosen toasty, burning Death Valley as the new hot spot for our love fests.

It's heating up. After a while the couple stands and in one last romantic gesture wrap their wings around each other. The music swells. His chest swells. Her chest swells. We turn away. I think I hear him give out a little moan.

Their Chief Complaint

WHEN THE EX-MARINE WALKS INTO THE CLINIC SHE SEES THAT, once again, he is in pain. His shoulders are hunched, his head bent over to the side, as if listening hard for a distant sound: a siren or a trumpet's call. His whole frame is collapsed in on itself, oddly curved—as if he's a contortionist who can will his body into pretzel shapes. At a carnival he'd fit right in with the sword swallowers and swamis, the snake charmers and midgets. He could draw a crowd. All he'd need is a barker, a shill to shout: "Step right up, ladies and gents. See the World's Most Twisted Man. As twisted as a grapevine! Two shows nightly!"

As his provider, she gets a ringside seat for every show. Each time he walks into the clinic the curtain rises. Along with him come his lovely assistants: his wife, the two sons, the daughter. They file in together like the Flying Wallendas, ready for their highwire act. After she examines him, she examines them. When he's out of the room she asks each to name his or her chief complaint. This is what they tell her:

He beats them. He beats them on a regular basis. He hits them when he is in pain. He is always in pain.

He is their chief complaint.

She asks him to get onto the exam table and disrobe. He takes off his sweat-shirt. Hatch marks cover his torso, a splatter of blue cross marks and holes. Xs and Os. His body is tattooed where the shrapnel went in, where shards from the exploding canister hit his body like small blows flying from out of nowhere.

She thinks again of his family, tries not to see cause and effect. That pain begets pain.

On the wall above the exam table is a framed copy of the Hippocratic Oath, a gift from her med school professor. As she takes his pulse she gazes at it and, as always, her eyes fall on the line *Above all, do no harm.* She's taken the oath to heart and believes pain is to be treated wherever she finds it. She finds it daily—in the junkie with the lost methadone script, in the guy who takes his Vicodin and sells it on the street. She tries not to judge the drunkard dying of liver failure, the young teenager knocked up, again. After she treats each patient she wipes her mind clean, like a math teacher preparing for the next class session, the blackboard erased, cleared of chalk markings. All the Xs and Os.

She always wanted to be a doctor. When she was seven her mother gave her a toy medicine kit. She opened her own clinic in an abandoned cardboard refrigerator box. *Open your mouth,* she'd say, as she pressed a Popsicle stick on her patients' tongues. She performed physicals on her brothers and sisters, on the young kids on the block. When she ran out of new patients her father suggested she turn to animals. He said that when he was a boy he sold cats to a Chinese restaurant. "Fifty cents a cat. There were so many cats I had extras."

"What about the ones you didn't sell?" she asked.

He said he played a game called "Poor, poor kitty." He swung them around by their tails. He put walnut shells on their paws and watched them try to walk.

She knew he must have had the shells set out in a neat line on the sidewalk, at the ready. He was obsessed with order, had always wanted everything just so; his slippers placed just so, his newspaper folded just so, his meal just so, the fork a specific distance from the plate, and everything was never just so, so there was a smack here and a smack there.

One afternoon, coming home from school, she walked in the front door and found him in the living room, gun in hand, pointed at her mother. She knew what to do in a crisis. She offered to get him another drink.

He said, "Why the hell not."

When she brought it back from the kitchen, filled to the brim, he lifted it to his lips, and drained half the glass. He placed the gun down on the glass table next to the chair. She remembers the sound of the metal hitting the glass top. Her mother stayed frozen, as if they were playing a game of Statue, as if she would stay in that position until someone tagged her and set her free.

He tossed back what remained of that drink. Then she brought another. She kept bringing them, refilling his glass, for even then she knew about remedies: how much soda, how much ice. When he passed out in the armchair, his arms and legs splayed, his body contorted, she quietly snatched the gun off the table and hid it in the basement, behind the washing machine.

That night, at dinner, they ate in silence. Not a word. There was only an occasional sound of the ice clinking against the side of his glass.

At the end of the meal, he looked over to her and gave an order.

"Clear the table."

Her mother didn't make a move.

She stood up and picked up her plate. Below it, on the tablecloth, something caught her eye. A torn slip of paper. She bent down to look closer, and scrawled across it were the words "Where is it?" She picked up her mother's plate, another note: "Give it back." Under her father's plate: "Now."

⚓ ⚓ ⚓

The ex-Marine is sitting on the edge of the exam table. She looks into his eyes. She wants to ask him when it all began. She wants him to tell her where, exactly, is the locus of pain. She wants to ask: *Where is it?*

He sits there, with his shirt off, shivering. She's tried everything that Western medicine has to offer. Nothing has worked. She has one last option for special cases. She can give him an acupuncture treatment. She asks if he is willing to try.

"Yes," he says, "yes. Anything, I will try anything."

He lays his body down on the exam table. She places needles in his shoulders, his neck, makes a pattern down his central spine. Around each needle, like a quick flame, a red area forms. A circle. A bull's eye. She knows this means the heat is releasing and will dissipate in a few minutes. She knows that other things will not dissipate.

For the treatment to work the needles must grab, make the connection. She turns the needles once, twice. He lets out a groan. She turns them again. Another groan.

She turns them again.

When she is finished his back looks like a carpet of tiny nails. A bed of nails. A swami could lie upon him to show his ability to transcend pain.

She could be that swami. She could lie down upon him, to get him to stop.

Step right up, shouts the barker.

Finally, she sees what she's been waiting to see. His shoulders drop down. His breathing deepens. Something is released. If only it were shrapnel rising to the surface of the skin, like a splinter surfaces, like a memory surfaces, to work its way out of the body, over time.

She leans down close, close to his ear and whispers.

"You have such beautiful children. Such a loving wife. "

He moves his head to say something and cries out when one of the needles shifts. After that, he stays still.

"They only think of you. They are so good to you," she says.

He is helpless. He cannot move.

"I can help. I can't make you well, but I can remove some of your pain."

He says nothing, yet she thinks she sees the slightest shift of his head, to hear better what she has to say.

"Here is the remedy," she whispers. "Treat them well. Cherish them. Love your family."

She plants this in him, a message that comes out of nowhere, like a shard or lines written on white paper that will work their way into his skin. He cannot deflect them.

Somewhere, someone pays the price of admission. Somewhere, a boy tosses a ring around a milk bottle and wins a prize. Somewhere, the swami succeeds.

The Raft

THEY ARE ALL ON THE RAFT AT THE BEGINNING, EVERYONE who ever counted in your life, along with those who didn't count, the resolved and the unresolved, every true blue friend, every nemesis, every good neighbor, every bad, your kindergarten teacher, the school bully, swim instructors, car mechanics of honest and ill repute, the quiet man you saw every morning at the coffee shop, who nodded as you entered, your favorite grocery checker who rounded off the total more than once, the shifty tax accountant, the girl who gave you your first kiss, the one who chose another, every inconsequential affair, and on there too, everyone of consequence, the inner circle, family, blood, those you call your loved ones, your one and only.

If you have evidence—credible, irrefutable—that the end is coming, if you have been given a timeline, then you have time to gather up everyone, see that they get on board, which isn't possible for those who are taken from this life without notice, off guard, quickly, in a flash, an instant, in the plane going down, or the car crash, the gunshot, the heart that bursts without warning; not possible for those who drop dead in their tracks, right there on the sidewalk, for no apparent reason, nothing to indicate today was the day of reckoning for them, the day of sorrow for those who didn't see it coming and therefore weren't able to go along for the ride. Their loved ones will never be able to make a case in their defense, propose a bargain—*Take me instead*—not like all those people on your raft who propose and propose and propose to no avail, who know full well that getting on board with you means somewhere, sometime, in the not too distant future, the ride will end.

So in the beginning it's like a party, or a convention of everyone you know or knew, and you've even invited the estranged, the long gone, the ones you've banished from your life, the grudge that never ended, the betrayal that never healed, that resulted in years of absence, in not calling, though, Lord knows, nowadays we always have the means within reach, you can ask the person in the grocery line, right in front of you, if they wouldn't mind, can you use their phone, and you can call because you remember the number, be honest, you remember, and when they answer, say *I just wanted to hear your voice again,* without initially telling them the kicker, that your days are numbered, are being tallied by someone with an abacus in hand, and each day, week, month, the hand reaches out and moves a bead over to the other side, and each time you hear the click of the wooden bead: loud, sharp, final.

You float down the river and soon learn this isn't a joy ride, you're not free yet, of duty, of care, of what binds you to the earth; there's one more job to do. It's your task to turf the unessential cargo. Certain people must go, and even though it was you who invited them along, it is now you who decides the ones who don't matter: the one-night stand, the members of the PTA, the odd relations you had to stomach but could just as well have done without—the convict nephew, the viperous aunt—and all the coworkers who came back late from their breaks and didn't care that you had to work over, and you were robbed of those minutes, precious minutes you could use now. How many minutes are wasted in waiting, in stewing, in unhappiness, and there are others who don't deserve a second thought, all the bosses who were, well, bosses, and therefore expendable when the time comes, for this is the one time the rank and file rise up and turn the tables, here's the real revolution, so you can say supervisor, and hey, you, CEO, you go first, and you give them a little push.

Now there's more room to move, not exactly a dance floor but a little more elbow room, and you begin to enjoy this spaciousness, this range of motion, now you can see the point of letting go, of getting rid of all that encumbers, and like a circus carney with his finger on the flip switch that, once flipped, sends the clown into the dunking tank, you are the one who gets to say when, and you laugh, not at the surprised look on the clown's face, or the way he flails underwater—glub, glub, glub—not at others' misfortune but at your own meager power, this little bit of say-so that's delicious and spiteful and then strangely sad; see, it's not meanness really, it's just that your body's getting weaker and you're less able to maneuver the raft with all that weight, so there goes the good friend who fed your dogs when you went on vacation, there goes the couple you played poker with, now a favorite schoolteacher who taught you the wonders of the Pleistocene, now a childhood priest.

You must jettison them one by one in order to stay longer, that's how it is, either or; you aren't able to carry them though, ironically, when they signed on they thought they were carrying you, they thought you were the one who needed help. They joined up to be there for your every need: to fluff a pillow, run errands, bring a tuna casserole, *Eat, eat,* they say, *you need to build your strength,* and you, who hate tuna, take a bite. All these people, well-meaning, telling you what to do, and it dawns on you that there's always a flip side: while they think they are the strong ones, the support, it's the other fucking way around, and you want to shout *I am carrying you,* but instead of wasting your voice, you pretend like you need to stretch and you make a grand sweep with your right arm and six go in at once, and because it's so easy, and ultimately economical, you do the same with your left arm and the raft almost tips over as one entire side falls off. (And you think to yourself, *This is a new form of triage,* and then continue.)

So it's you and you and you and you. With quick speed you decide, you whittle and reduce and bring the number down. Now you can count the ones who are left on one hand. You've been efficient, and they stand before you, staring your way: your mother, your sister, your father, who is dead, your one and only. Push your father over first; you'll see him soon, he's already on the other side, so you explain the deal: it's kind he came, but let's meet up later, and he gives a knowing smile as he was the first to teach you how to leave, and then does a swan dive and hardly makes a splash. Now whose turn, it's harder to decide, but you choose your mother, who bore you and raised you, who failed you as you failed her, *I'm sorry,* you tell her, *sorry we were never able to ford the distance but even so I've been meaning to tell you thank you for all you did, but on the other hand, why did it have to be so hard,* and before she goes she holds your hand for a moment and because you are diminished, because you have been getting smaller all this time, your hand feels small in hers, as it must have felt when you were young, and you feel the warmth of her body pressed into the flesh, into the palm of her hand, pressed into you, and then, without warning, you let go.

Your sister's next, whom you only came to know, to really know, late in life, whom you'll never know, not like when you were young: an older sister who looked after you, who put her hands on your shoulders as if you were a pet and steered you through tall crowds, who handed you down her outgrown clothes—her red blazer with the gold buttons, the blazer you coveted, that had her smell, her power. She's been there the whole trip, with her cheery stories and Hallmark cards and silly gifts that you cherish—the cat holding on in the TGIF poster, the pop psychology books on how to create your destiny—each gift as precious as a hand-made basket or a requiem. It will be hard for her, for she will have no one left, for even though there is her husband, her children, they aren't first blood; a father long gone from this world into another, a mother long gone in this life, and you her only link, and that's why you push her, tenderly over the side, for you cannot lift her any longer, and she, even though she never knew it, she, for so long, by her pluck and belief and good heart, has lifted you.

There's only one left. The one. Your one. You decide, right then, to never let go. You will take her with you, you'll strap her on board and you can go together, it will be like a weekend away, you tell her, a chance for a little break, a trip up the Mendocino coast, a drive to the country. You were lucky, so very lucky, you loved her and she loved you, and face it, she is the one whose hands built this very raft, with her knowledge of tools and craft, she was always the practical one, and it was she who packed the picnic basket and looked after provisions, she told the doctors when to intervene and when to go to hell, she made the passenger list and rowed when your arms were too tired. She took care of everything so you could save your strength, so you could push the others over, she made it all possible for you to leave like this, in full command, possible to leave this life without regret, for you felt loved by her. You're not sure if she can swim without you. Someone else can teach her, it's high time she learned. And, when her back is turned, you give her the most loving, the firmest push and she falls into the waves.

There is no one left; there's room to stretch and move. Room for a game of foursquare or calisthenics, room for cartwheels, forward rolls, pirouettes. Funny this lightness you feel, this expansive body, no one to bump into, no burden to carry. They're gone, all your loved ones and those not so loved, they're gone and what's odd is you don't miss them, for you are past that, with them went all feeling: blame, regret, love, sorrow, anger. Once the bodies left, so did the pain. Every bead on the abacus is carried over to the one side, except one. There's one more thing that needs to go. You have to jettison this, even this, the raft, sturdy raft, life raft, and in an instant it breaks in two, so flimsy, like a cardboard box, it falls away. How did it ever stand your weight, how did it ever hold you?

About the Author

TONI MIROSEVICH GREW UP IN EVERETT, WASHINGTON, IN A Croatian-American fishing family, which was part of an extensive Slav immigrant community. She received her M.A. and her M.F.A. in creative writing at San Francisco State University. Her first book of poetry and prose, *The Rooms We Make Our Own* (Firebrand Books), was published in 1996. Her award-winning work has appeared in numerous literary journals and magazines, including *The Kenyon Review, Puerto del Sol, Harrington Lesbian Fiction Quarterly, San Francisco Chronicle Magazine,* and *Western Humanities Review,* and in anthologies such as *The Impossible Will Take a Little While* (Basic Books, 2004), *Revenge and Forgiveness* (Henry Holt, 2004), *Best American Travel Writing 2002* (Houghton Mifflin), and *The Discovery of Poetry* (Harcourt, 2001). Custom Words published *Queer Street* in 2005. Ms. Mirosevich has also published two chapbooks: *My Oblique Strategies* (Thorngate Road, 2005), which received the Frank O'Hara Chapbook Award, and *Trio: Toni Mirosevich, Charlotte Muse, Edward Smallfield* (Specter Press, 1995).

Ms. Mirosevich teaches at San Francisco State University.

< 203 >